Back to Mississippi

Sidewalks represent a journey to the paths of my success, follow my steps and take the journey!

Geraldine Edwards Hollis

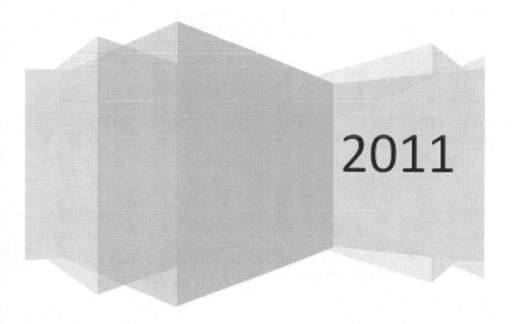

2011

Library of Congress Control Number: 2011916747
ISBN: Hardcover   978-1-4653-6822-5
               Softcover   978-1-4653-6821-8
               Ebook   978-1-4653-6823-2

To order additional copies of this book, contact:
Xlibris Corporation
1-888-795-4274
www.Xlibris.com
Orders@Xlibris.com
105070

TABLE OF CONTENTS

Dedication

In all things and in all ways I am Thankful for the Reality of this Documentation of the life experiences that has brought me to this time and place in My Life. You made it possible!

Thy will be done! Amen.

Acknowledgement

To acknowledge my team is to honor what has been given to me. This project of documenting my memories has been a task of a higher magnitude than any other writing that I have experienced. All of my life work has been in some form of a team, group and most of all living in a cohesive family. To successfully get this manuscript where it is now has been a team action. This group of individuals has genuinely helped me because they wanted to make sure my story was shared and that it was in a form that could be understood for generations to come. To do this took patience on my part and ongoing growth. I had to open up and bare some things that were not easy for me to do. It is still hard for me to talk about so much that happened to me especially in my youth and young adult life. I am thankful for my supporters, and all of you who read my story.

About ten years before starting to seriously write, I found a friend who I encouraged to be with me and never let me give in or give up on my dreams. We both agreed to support each other with the love of a friend, and the force of a strong kick. We both have strong personalities. Today, I am happy to say that friend stayed true to our agreement. Without true friendship, dedication and compassion this project would not be what it is. I am appreciative of her and all of my supportive team.

First, I am grateful for life. The adversity in my life made living a big challenge. I am thankful for my life partner, friend and husband, JH. He has watched over me as I made life changes, and encouraged my progress, to share. He monitored me because he wanted to keep me from over working both physically and emotionally. We learned that this can happen when you are on a writer's run! It is hard to stop when your mind is focused in the emotions. There have been many long days and nights that went past midnight. Altogether the work days have been far too many to count. All along the days and nights, there has been a team member supporting my efforts.

The readers who read my first *completed* manuscript, were encouraging despite my mostly pages of facts. What they read was my proclamation of raw memories that I finished writing on 12/31/10. I made a milestone in my first draft and had a shock when the process of editing began and lasted forever. There was the time when I lost some chapters because of a computer glitch and could not retrieve the written words. Because they were mostly facts, I was able to rewrite them.

The readers read over and over never complaining as they encouraged me even more. They shared the pro and cons and never wavered, continuing to be an inspiration to me.

Not all team members read as a part of the experience. Some gave good advice even in the beginning to get me started on the road to being an author. Some worked on the graphics for the exterior as well as the interior of the finished book. A lot of time and effort went into making this product successful by everyone. All that I can really say is, Thanks!

I say thank you for all that you unselfishly gave of your influence, time and talent to help, support and assist me in getting this product where it is now! For your editing and encouraging style for the duration, I am so grateful. There were many who just wanted to be a blessing and you were. To Thelma Hollis Nutting and DeEtter Wyatt Edwards, for reading and proofreading, I am happy to have you on my literary team but also my lifelong team. To publisher, Ronald Howard who gave such specific advice in the beginning of the project even as he was busy writing for a new book and movie. To Lawrence Gray, a publisher in my community group, for help with insight into formatting and encouraging words. To a friend of a friend, for keeping up with my progress and giving input in the beginning chapters but could not continue due to personal reasons, I am thankful for what was done. Jackie Navielle Nutting, my granddaughter, is so special to me. She gave us her talent in the three sketches of me at those times in my life. For the specially designed covers, I give credit for the dynamic friendship and consultant services of Dr. Richard Clark.

In the final process, I am most grateful for a young lady that I have known since she was a student of mine for the first teaching years at Madison Junior High School. (MJHS) in Oakland, CA; Claudia Lajoyce Gardley has been sharing her skills as proofreader and also a promoter to let fellow classmates of hers know about the book. Her awesome enthusiasm has been infectious and more than welcomed. Members of the Northern California Alumni Chapter, Ministers and Community United, Inc. and The Love Circle Mission of First Baptist Church, I received much from all of you. Big thanks to those who continued to encourage me along the way. I give continued praise of thanks to my friend and sometime foe, the one who has guided this process with love and preciseness all along the editorial part of the product. I am more than grateful for her steadfastness and patience with me as we moved from phase to phase and not always smoothly, but always with the main focus clearly outlined for me to see. The vision, knowledge and directions are what has made this project what it really is. Her directions and guidance kept all phases moving forward. Again I say, thanks for a job well done.

To all of the team members and especially my life friend and husband, I am forever grateful for your support and being a part of the, *Back to Mississippi* team.

Introduction

It has been asked many times, "How did it feel to do what you did on March 27, 1961?" There is no simple answer.

Many people may have read the popular magazines and newspapers of the time to learn facts of what happened with a group that became known as the *Tougaloo Nine*. Their actions propelled Mississippians to a place that they were unwilling to go. There was no recourse. A fierce momentum started as surely as any event and any challenge before or since that time. Imagine, a few black students, from a small Christian college in a town with a name even unfamiliar to many Mississippians. Now, imagine the situation when a group of whites who were known as the *Sovereignty Commission* found *the world on their steps to the Jackson, Mississippi White only Library*. The media world was there looking at them as they maneuvered this non-violent event with guns, dogs, and officers. In fact, there were about two officers for each of these nine black students. There was fear, intimidation, and outrage portrayed to think that these blacks, *Negros'* had the audacity to invade their domain.

These are the facts but now let me tell you that only God knows what happened to me. My feelings are locked away in memory; still there waiting to *escape*. However, even bottled up in my guts, my very being needs to be free. I needed to be acknowledged.

I felt the need of acceptance for the evidence of a life lived well in spite of the challenges that propelled me on this journey of dynamic *change*.

For me, dialog and journaling tell the insights of my thinking, prior to finding myself selected as a member of the group that represented Mississippi in a way that opened the closed society of human kind as never seen before. What a predicament! This show of civil disobedience, this act, peaceful and cooperative as it was, diminished the superiority of the governing body of this great state. How dare these young blacks to act on their belief of equal status and behave in such an unexpected attitude of compliance as they, were escorted out of the library. There were the tools to quell violence ready to put the Nine in their place for breaking the laws of suppression, degradation and second—class citizenry. Their actions of non-violence were a big disappointment of the powerful protectors of this Superior State of Mississippi!

The story that follows is my attempt to let my memories escape, for my sake and for yours. My desire is that you build on my goals and sacrifices to continue to use all that you are to make this a better world for all humanity.

Who am I? I am someone who lived most of my formative years in the segregated state of Mississippi. I am a citizen molded during the mid-twentieth century in the state of Mississippi. I am a part of the first young black adults to breach the forbidden entry into a public library in Jackson, Mississippi. Library entrance would have been tolerated as a janitor, but not as a library patron. This happened early in 1961, before any other group action and started the spiral of civil disobedience in Mississippi. We started this eventual escalation and it did not stop even with the stand made by then, Governor Ross Barnett. Nine students made this historical move. I was one of those nine students from a college in Tougaloo, Mississippi, given a name of distinction, The Tougaloo Nine.

My name is Geraldine Edwards. In 1961, I was in my second year at Tougaloo Christian College, Tougaloo Mississippi. What I did at that time is a part of who I am. What I did at that time gave all men, women, boys and girls the opportunity and constitutional right to live their lives with the right to vote. To vote without the Poll Tax and without intimidating oral questions.

Tougaloo may not have been as well known as some of the other Historical Black Colleges. However, it was a Mecca for higher learning, where excellence was the expectation. Tougaloo always stressed living and being the best you could be. Tougaloo excelled by being an outstanding educational institution. During the years of my attendance '59 to '62, the college had the most diverse faculty I have ever seen in such a small institution. Most teachers and staff lived on the campus and we knew they were there for us. There was so much to love about the Tougaloo Christian College experience. Tougaloo College was and still is more than that. Tougaloo excels by being an outstanding educational institution.

Tougaloo was a rallying point, for celebrities and for, Civil Rights Proponents of all races, creeds and colors. Tougaloo was a spot where strategies, meetings and everything else took place in the Sociology Lab on the campus for discussion, planning and networking. This was a part of the process before any actions, were implemented off campus. I remember when many whose names evade my recall, visited the campus. When any of these political activists came to the gates of the campus, they felt secure. Tougaloo College was a safe haven for Social Change Agents. We were elements of this justice driven surroundings.

This is my justification and memory of how I became a member of the Historical Tougaloo Nine. As the saying goes, *if you do not know your history, you are prone to repeat it*! As you read my life experiences, put yourself in my place. No matter what kind of life you live, envision being me. Feel my experiences, journey with me as I move through various neighborhoods, schools and states. One of the things that I want to show is that I was blessed to be here to tell you about my journey. Travel with me and my family as we give positive insights into the life that was ours. Remember, I am not bitter or angry but grateful for the opportunity to say that I made a difference for those of you who came behind me and for those of you who will succeed me.

As you read my life's journey, ask yourself how you would have handled the segregation, degradation, second class citizenship, degraded educational materials, jail and the circumstances that threatened our families.

Everyone has a history. As I ponder, and pull from my memories from so many years ago, I wonder if this will become a history to be embraced. When you know your history, you do not have to repeat it. When I made choices in the Tougaloo Nine Event, it was to build individuals and society, both socially and economically.

Remembering that as we live, our today becomes our yesterday and our tomorrow becomes our today. It has been my goal to live each day in the present. Yesterday is gone and really tomorrow is not promised. As we live we should have a reason for the results of our life. To have a purpose, goal or ideal for making things better for our community, family and humankind in general. This is a noble cause that sometimes comes with pain, hardship or even disappointment. If you are blessed, as I know I am, you have gratitude and thanksgiving for making a difference for others, even if they do not know it or even acknowledge it.

Prologue:The Journey Begins from When my memory of what Was, Surfaced.

Prologue

Back to Mississippi . . . July 09, 2008

JH drove at the speed limit. The posted 65mph gave us a comfortable ride on Highway 61, the newly finished four-lane. We were enjoying the rolling green hills, the creeping vines and the pine trees pointing to the clear and almost cloudless sky. It was sunny, a bit hot and very humid. We felt all of this as we floated down the roadway on waves of heat vapors. We got the same feelings because that was how it was when we stopped at a gas station just north of Baton Rouge, Louisiana. Our trip so far had been pleasant and steady. We glided along as content as we could be. We made the usual stops, driving from morning until dusk with occasional breaks. We made fill-up and pit-stop releases at gas stations and highway rest stops. This gave us the opportunity to interact with other drivers and to see where they were traveling from and where they were going. They in turn alerted us to road conditions, the visibility of the Highway Patrol Officers and State Troopers. It also provided a bit of social interaction. There is just so much you can do on some stretches of the roadway. There is selective radio, your cache of CDs and limited cell phone conversations.

When you travel without children, you have some peace but you can really appreciate the unexpected out of the blue questions that they ask, all along the entire length of the driving route. The unexpected questions that they ask are sometimes a break from the tenseness of the drive. The expected conversations are sometimes stares, expressions or not what you would like to hear when travelling with children. "Where are we?" or "when are we going to get there?" may be placed where you may expect something educational, geological and even botanical because of the change in the species of trees and grasses.

North of Baton Rouge, from the roadside it seemed that we were out in the middle of no-man's land. There was not a business or attraction there to take away your attention. As we sped along, and crossed the state line from Louisiana, JH read the border sign aloud. The sign boldly stated, "It's like coming home!" I do not know what it was, but this sign made a difference this time. It was at this time that I seriously started thinking, writing and searching from within to find out why this time was different. On the one hand, the sign made assumptions that everyone who left the state of Mississippi did so with regrets. On the other hand, it implied that the circumstances were so very nurturing while living there previously, that they were coming back to a great occasion. For some of us that was not the case. JH and I came back out of duty, devotion and love of our families whom we left back in 1968. We were thankful that God blessed us to be able to make the trip as frequently as we did. Our extended family did not have the financial means or opportunity to visit us. When we visited them, we had good healthy food, fellowship, extensive extended families and love.

I really enjoyed the formative years that I spent in Mississippi. I was grateful because my family moved to Mississippi to give all of us a better financial life from the ones we had, when we lived in Louisiana and Texas. However, it is so important that I share the family togetherness, love and adventure of staying at my grandparents' home in Vidalia, Louisiana. Living there before we moved to Mississippi were the happiest years of my life. I realize it now and I want to acknowledge it. Happiness is not always in what you can purchase or where you live! The focus of this happiness will come at a later time because I want to share it with you. Even as an adult, I feel very drawn to living around or near the place I left before my family first moved to Mississippi. At the very pinnacle of this feeling is a desire to replicate the core of living that was provided to all of our family by granddad and the one I recognize as grandma on both my maternal and paternal sides. Her name, Mrs. Texanna White, known as Mama Tex and was also called Grandma X2 when we wrote about her.

This special grandma taught me much about life. She taught me to cook when I was a girl of seven. She taught me how to forage for wild greens and berries. She taught me to use our increase in fruit and vegetables to share with others by preserving, making jelly, jam and even wine. Elderberry bushes grew in abundance on the fences along the back of our property and was said to be inedible. But not so in Mama Tex hands. She made the best jam and wine out of those clusters of dark blue berries that I have ever tasted!

To get wild greens she showed me how to go out into the fields with only a butter knife and a sack to collect *dandelions*. I later learned that they are some of the healthiest of green vegetables. The dandelions grow flat to the ground with very large leaves. You needed the butter knife, to cut the greens from the root. Mama Tex told us, "that the dandelion has just one heck of a long tough root that we had to whack a certain way so the leaves would grow back for another meal."

Mama Tex, believed in natural holistic remedies. She taught me to identify and to use many herbs and plants. One of the reasons for telling you this is because I had many ailments and Mama Tex took care of me and my entire family. I only remember going to the doctor twice when I was growing up. In second grade the teacher found out that I could not see the blackboard so I went to the eye doctor for testing. The other ailment Mama Tex could not cure was a throat infection that gave me frequent sore throats and bad breath. My mom took me to the doctor and I had a tonsillectomy at the General Hospital in Natchez, Mississippi for this. I convalesced or rather recuperated in the colored wing of the hospital. The best part of my stay and the part I remember most was all of the ice cream, gelatin and puddings that I got to eat. This was a rare opportunity to eat fun food because it was nutritious.

After that, during all of my childhood development, I had no bad health or indications of any kind of health problems. This was thanks to the awesome home garden and cooking of wholesome meals at our family home for the duration of my childhood. Today, I am an advocate for wellness and daily healthy eating. Not a purist, not a vegan or a vegetarian but one who lives life, fit and well.

Part 1:
The Beginning of the Destination, Getting to Mississippi.

Chapter 1

From Vidalia to Orange to Vidalia to Natchez.

Vidalia was across the mighty Mississippi River from Natchez, Mississippi. A great little town and it was my place of happy memories. This small town is on the west side of the Mississippi River. My mother was the third child and the second girl born to Alfred and Alicia White. She and I were both born in Vidalia, Louisiana.

Mom met Dad in 1940 on the Mississippi River Bridge. At the time the bridge was two lanes and used as much for walking as it was for driving. Vidalia was like a subdivision to Natchez. All of the major shopping and entertainment for Vidalia was in Natchez or Ferriday, Louisiana, where Dad was living at the time they met. Mom and a friend were walking in one direction. Dad and a friend walked on the other side of the bridge along on the edge of the ridge. He bet his friend that he could talk to her. I do not know if the other guy got the other girl but Dad was successful. They were very compatible and they connected. They both came from hard working families and they had the commonality of having worked in the fields and wanting to escape that lifestyle. They had a courtship, marriage and then I was born. Dad was inducted into the Army. Mom stayed in the family home on Spruce Street in Vidalia, while my Dad served in World War II. My brother Pete was born during those span of years.

I remember vividly, that it was during this time that Grandmother Alicia became very ill with congestive heart failure. I did not know what it was because I was a toddler and she could no longer pick me up or hold me. Granddad worked and Mom had the responsibility of keeping the household running. There were her two young children to care for, me and my infant baby brother. My father's mother, Texanna came to Vidalia to help take care of Grandmother Alicia. She was a natural born caregiver who went from home to home taking care of sick individuals. Here too is where I find myself in the same mentality. I have established a history of care giving to others throughout my life. My younger brothers were the first to whom I gave care. If you are the first born, this role of being a caregiver is one of the responsibilities that come naturally. Especially if you are a girl and boys make up the rest of the family.

Dad was given an Honorable Discharge from the army and came back home to Vidalia. Soon after he was settled back home, he found there were jobs in Texas. We packed up and moved to Orange, Texas. We were a new family of four, Dad, Mom, Pete and me. The move was only for a few years to take advantage of the abundant work in the oil fields in Port Arthur, Texas. After two years, we moved back to Vidalia and to the family home on Spruce Street. I started school in Orange before our move back to Louisiana. After our return to Vidalia, we started a new family life once again. I went to school in Vidalia, which was my second school experience. Later we moved to Mississippi where I completed my formal education.

It was during the time we were away from Vidalia in Orange, Texas, that my grandmother Alicia died. My granddad, Alfred married my dad's mother. She became Mama Tex to all of us. It is always a little confusing to some of my friends when I share how my Grandma Texanna, was my grandmother two times over. She was my father's mother, and married my mother's father, Alfred. My grandfather was now my father's step-father while my mother was the step-daughter of Mama Tex. Two sets of parents in one marriage. Did you get it?

Cohesive family togetherness is something that Mama Tex, instilled in us because of how she cared for individuals and all of the family in general. She was the one who kept both sides of the family connected. She kept the community connected when she went to sit with others in sickness and times of need. Today whenever I volunteer I know that this is where it all started for me. We must get to Mississippi where this story is leading.

By the way, I enjoy leading! But found that what I really do is now called facilitation. As I progressed, lived and learned, my ideal outlook on life was set in place by my Mama Tex. She was my first leader and inspired me to be curious. To do things that was not always the norm, essentially, to take initiative and not be afraid to lead. She taught me to live and to thrive. Not just survive.

To get to Mississippi, the journey starts in 1950. We had to leave Vidalia where my grandmother Texanna and my granddad Alfred, lived. Remember, they married each other after my mom's mother died. It was an arranged marriage. My maternal grandmother, Alicia told my granddad to marry Texanna, because she was a good and caring woman. My granddad had a younger handicapped daughter, who was in high school and needed to have a mother. My grandmother Alicia knew she would not make it and knew that she needed to look out for the well-being of the family. So she made preparations by getting granddad Alfred and Mama Tex together. They had to be married, because it was not Christian practice for women and men to live together without the benefit of *marriage*!

Granddad Alfred was an outstanding man in the community. It best served our family, that he had a reputable wife. Granddad was a deacon in the Zion Baptist Church. He was a trustee and took care of many of the support duties as a Leader in the congregation. He was not a sharecropper, nor a cotton picker, hoer, or field hand. He was a supervisor for Mr. Matthews who owned the cotton fields in the north end of Vidalia. My granddad was also the oldest in his family of twelve siblings. He drove the truck for the landowner to and from the fields where many of his brothers sharecropped. They all lived in housing provided by the land owners. But my granddad owned his land. His property consisted of three lots, taking up over half of a block. There he provided his family with food, animals, a home and a barn with orchards of fruit on each side of the house. It was a totally self-sustaining small working farm.

After our return back to Vidalia, there were three families in the house. Mom, dad, Pete, along with brothers John born in Orange, baby Ezelle born in Vidalia and myself were one family. Aunt Chris was a single parent and she had a boy, Willie and soon a baby girl, Joyce. Grandmother Texanna had her daughter's daughter, Rosie and her grandson, William, whom we all called Bill, living with us along with Granddad. There were five adults, two teens, and six children under the age of ten living together and making a home on Spruce Street in Vidalia.

I did not know all of my cousins in Vidalia and never got to know all of them because there were so many. My granddad had eleven other siblings and most of the brothers lived in Vidalia. He was the oldest of the twelve so some of the brothers' children were my age. Grandfather's family name is White. The White family came from a plantation named, *White Hall.* Everybody in Vidalia was kinfolk. At any rate that's the way it seemed. There were uncles, aunts, cousins and more cousins. I never did get to know who was who until 2008, when the White Family had their, *First of Many Reunions* there in Vidalia, Louisiana.

The house on Spruce Street had six rooms which included the kitchen and a dining room. This was the center of the house for eating, socializing and even the canning of foods. The dining room was larger than any other room in the house and was equipped with a large sturdy round table with a capacity to seat all of the family at one time. There were built-in cabinets and food storage areas. Essentially the dining area was also our pantry. There were three bedrooms and a front room which served as living, entertainment, and sleeping area for two of my brothers and me. The front room was the main entrance and included a couch, chairs, and a radio console that we listened to while lying on the floor in front of it. There was a table with family photos. Pictures hung on the wall. The area was very functional and the bed in the corner served as sitting space in the daytime.

In Vidalia I could ride a bike all over the black portion of town which was on the north side where we lived. I was familiar with the downtown residential area south of town where other black family members lived but did not venture over there because of the busy main street. The town's shopping area ran parallel along the highway that ran through it from east of the river to west towards Ferriday. All of the *white* folks lived closer to the town with sidewalks in front of their homes. If Vidalia was a circle, the downtown would be in the center. The white citizens lived in the areas surrounding the downtown area. The outer larger area would be where the black citizens lived away from the development of both sidewalks and paved streets. The residential area for blacks had ditches in front of their properties and gravel in the streets. It was so dusty! The town's maintenance department would spray the streets with oil every summer. This procedure only kept the dust down to a minimum, which meant that the spraying had to be done regularly, and it was. Summer evenings also found the crew going around the black residential area spraying some kind of dark heavy smoke, *for the mosquitoes*. Now, this was only in the black residential area. If you can see where I am going with this, just nod your head!

In front of the home, along the fences were dirt paths instead of sidewalks. Between the dirt paths and the graveled streets were deep ditches. Remember there were no sidewalks in the plan. What a dangerous passageway we had to travel. When it rained it was muddy. When it did not rain it was a cushion of loose dirt, just like talcum powder.

The ditch in front of my granddads home was our *green* playground. In rainy weather, we had an ecological paradise. We were able to observe frog eggs grow into tadpoles and eventually into frogs. We would catch them in tin cans and watch their progress from our close up *microscopic* view. It was an enlightening experience. Whenever it rained the ditch filled with water and ran towards the river. The four foot long bridge across the ditch was our play station as we watched the water flow under the bridge and around the trunk of the large weeping willow tree. The ditches allowed us to have fun as we used our environment for learning. They were dangerous, unsafe, and unsanitary, because they carried the wastewaters from the sidewalks and gutters in front of the *white folk's homes.* We did not associate the lack of sidewalks and sewage in our neighborhood as discrimination. That was just how it was for the folks who lived in the *black* sections of town.

The weeping willow trees had many uses. Medically, its bark was chewed to relieve pain. When being disciplined, they used its branches for our spankings, of which I got many. The flexible branches were used in making and repairing furniture. When a Willow tree felled or a branch cut for any good reason, it was burned for warmth. It is a fast growing species tree and the ditches were perfect and fertile for its growth. There were two types of trees that I remember vividly, the willows that grew along the ditches in the area and the popular tree, which was called *China Ball.*

Being the first child and the only girl of my mother's children may have been a challenge to some but for me it was right in my comfort zone. I started going to school in Orange, Texas in first grade and was in the beginning of second grade when my dad brought us back home to our grandparents' home in Vidalia.

It was in October, when we arrived in Vidalia because it was Halloween the first day we arrived. I remember this very vividly because at the age of seven, I was covered in a sheet and allowed to run around with the older cousins as we went from house to house singing out, *trick or treat*. We had no collection bags and gladly received any treat we were given. The fun was just being out at dark, looking scary and going from door or rather house to house. It was so much fun. There was no candy or goodie bags like the ones children have today. There were no scary plastics or commercialized objects such as the ones big businesses promote and are taken for granted today. We simply donned a sheet, or put on some old clothes, like hats or even oversized overalls. We put make-up on our faces from our parent's dressers. It was all simple fun. This was my very first Halloween event and it was very memorable.

I started class in the second grade that November 1948. Two male cousins were in class with me. Both were my mom's first cousins. There may have been more because there were cousins that lived uptown and downtown. The school was in the downtown area which meant that the area was up from the main street where the town businesses were located and south down from the town area. The town area consisted of just the main street and the block to the north of the main street. The downtown included the courthouse, post office and a few other stores. A bank was on the corner of the main street. Black citizens had to walk longer distances just to get to the downtown or uptown depending on what side of town they lived.

As black students we had a challenge to get to our *schools*. That was an adventure in maneuvering all by itself. We had no choice in the matter. There were no city buses, or school buses and rarely any cars in the family. Public transportation did not exist. In Vidalia, we were called Colored or Negros at that time. The school was from first grade to twelfth grade and in two buildings. The elementary wing was a two story structure that was on the front of the school property.

The high School and all of the other grades for blacks in Vidalia was, Vidalia High School. The white students attended Vidalia High School on the north side. I had to go to school on the south side, not by choice but because of the segregation of races. By this time, I was accustomed to traveling around alone and trying new things. The downtown main street which is the road that runs through the town is Highway 84. As a highway it goes across the Mississippi River. It was the dividing line of demarcation for the schools. As a young girl of seven and eight years of age I had to cross this highway daily. If my cousin was not along with me I had to cross it alone.

The high school building housed the principal's office and the place from where the Federal Food Meals were delivered to the classrooms. Students' food came in # 10 cans brought to the classrooms to be served to students for lunch. I do not remember if the food was hot or what was served but I do remember that it cost twenty five cents for the week. It was food that I did eat and it was different from the beans and greens that were our usual food at home.

There were three buildings at our school, if you count the large outhouse without windows on the southwest of the campus. One end of the outhouse building, the one nearest the high school was for the girls. The other end, the side farthest from the main building was for the boys, the side farthest from the main building. The outhouses were today's restrooms without plumbing. The inside of the outhouses consisted of a row on both sides with a hole cut out in the plank that was your commode or personal usage seat! About ten people could sit on each side. There were no partitions and no privacy. Everyone sat on the hole and did their business: #1 or #2. There was a light in the ceiling and I think there was toilet paper, but we could have used old magazines' and newspapers. There were faucets for running water several places on campus. I do not remember there being soap to wash your hands. The time was the late 1940's. I do not believe that the white students had outhouses on their campus.

While in Vidalia, I learned two quite dangerous activities. I learned to skate, using my shoes. I would put the skates on and adjust the metal clips that screwed in to fit with the shoes on my feet. Then I would adjust metal to the length of the shoes on my feet. This was why I could use the hand-me down skates that were there at the house. When I wanted to go skating, I had to walk down towards town several blocks to the sidewalks, where I just had to put the skates on. My goal was the courthouse because it had sidewalks all around it. I would walk carefully up and down the steps in my skates on all four sides of the courthouse to challenge myself, because I could do it. I skated around without anyone saying anything to me. I completed the entire square before heading back north and home to my grandparent's house. There were always sidewalks where the white citizens lived. It is always amazing how blatant it was that only the white areas had sidewalks!

There were blacks living on both sides of town, but there were only dirt paths and ditches in front of their properties. No one saw this as an issue or at least no one complained or challenged the issue. I remember letting my parents know that we should have sidewalks like the white area. I was one of the ones who acknowledged this because I enjoyed skating, but I had to go so far in order to just put on my skates. As a youngster of seven, I usually went alone, without fear of bodily harm. I skated until it was getting dark or until I was tired or hungry.

My other activity was to ride my Cousin Bill's bicycle. Bill was a teenager, and his bike was twenty six inches, but I would take his bike whenever I got the chance. My legs would not reach the pedals on the large bicycle unless I started from a step or some other high place. But I found a way to get going. Stopping was also a challenge because I had to coast to a step or some other high place to safely stop. I do believe that I was not always 100% successful. I was determined to master this bicycling and I did just that. With experience, kinesthetic sense and balance, I learned to start on my right leg and move my body so that I could get on the bike. I had to move so that my leg could touch the pedals when it was up on each leg and push down to repeat this movement on the other side. I learned to slow down and eventually jump off of the bike to stop. I could not sit on the seat; I was on the pedals and in motion the majority of the time.

I must confess, I may have bruised myself, but I took good care of Bill's bike. He did not just allow me to ride it; I took advantage when he was not around. I was careful; I did not want to get into trouble with him. I enjoyed the freedom that the bike allowed me. I was free, alone, mobile and young in age, but older in determination. My goal was to do what I did, ride that bike and not break my neck or any limbs. If no one followed, it was not a problem. I chose to make decisions and to follow them to the desired goal. Yes, later in life I realized that this character trait helped me to develop into the individual I would eventually become.

Chapter 2

Natchez, Mississippi

In 1950, my Dad finished the courses he was attending in the Veteran Educational Program on the GI Bill, where he learned how to build his own home. He also got a job in Natchez at the International Paper Mill and started a project to build a home for his family.

When we moved to Natchez in 1951, our family had to live with my mother's brother and his wife on Daisy Street. My Aunt and Uncle did not have children and lived in a two bedroom, one bath home that they built just over a year before we moved in that fall. At that time there were five children in my family. My grandfather gave all of us a nickname when we were young. He had a name to fit some part of our characteristic. I was called Frog and Pete, with a given name of Simuel, found himself being called, Bo Pete. A brother five years younger named John, was called Johnny Boy. He was born in Orange, Texas when we lived there. A brother seven years younger than I was called Easy but his name was Ezelle. Then there was a baby brother at that time named Noel, but called Norah, who was three months old. Granddad gave each child in the house a nickname. Thankfully, all of our nicknames did not follow us to Natchez.

The reason we moved to my aunt and uncle's in Natchez, was because my parents wanted us to get started in school early before our new home would have been livable. We stayed on Daisy Street until around October before moving into our own home. On Daisy Street Mom and Dad and the two youngest kids stayed in the second bedroom. My two brothers next to me and I slept in the living room on the fold down couch and on a cot. This new subdivision where my aunt and uncle lived had sewage and indoor plumbing. There were no sidewalks and no ditches to play in. The street was over two blocks long but was not designed for an outlet or a turn-around. It was narrow. Almost everyone on Daisy Street drove a car. When you drove down Daisy Street, you drove into your driveway and backed out to turn back to the subdivision entrance. One reason that there was no outlet is the well known bayous. Natchez has bayous all over on the north side of town.

The bayous are an ecological paradise, and promote some of the best vegetation, wild berries and fruits. At their center was a stream with sand and gravel. Vines grew from the trees along the sides of the huge gorge in the earth. The bayous were also very dangerous. Our bayou caved in and residents used the garbage to fill in the cave-ins. This was dangerous in that there was broken furniture, glass and rusting cans that flowed down to the edge of the center of the bayou. Unsanitary objects also went down in the land fill. We did not know the danger. We children knew that parents warned us about playing in the bayou but being kids, we did it anyway. Many children have died in the deep ponds by drowning. Some were even bitten by the snakes and spiders which could have been fatal. But the mystical power drew the adventurous to its cool and shady belly on hot Mississippi days.

Bayous were fun and adventurous, and were meeting places for many of the children who lived on both sides of the bayou. As children we played on the bottom. It was like a park. Houses were built with their backs to the bayou on both sides. The bayous were an extension of the back yards. There were limited places to play and no park or playground except at the school much farther away.

Moving to Natchez, Mississippi meant that I was in a new town and had to attend a new school. Natchez was much larger than Vidalia. I had to learn my way around, maneuver the longer streets, the connecting alleys and even had to walk through a cemetery to get to certain streets. This school change and the larger town made it an adventure. But we were much farther from sidewalks than in Vidalia because Natchez was much larger. So I did not have the opportunity to skate anymore.

The school that I had to attend in Natchez was completely to the south east of the downtown area. It was probably 4 or 5 miles from Daisy Street to *Brumfield School* which went from grades 1 to 12. The school was one large two-story building. There were sidewalks around the school and all along St. Catherine Street all the way to Pine Street to the north of town. Where we lived on Daisy and eventually on Ray Street could be accessed from North Pine Street. When we turned off of Pine Street at Steers Lane to travel to Daisy and also to Ray Street we had no more sidewalks to walk on to and from our daily activities. We had a lot of gravel or dirt paths to tread and partly in the street. It was very unsafe walking even for adults.

I started in the 5th grade and my teacher was great. Her name is one I related to all of my life also, it was Mrs. Theresa Lewis.

I learned so very much in her class. In fact, it was her idea to bring home made candies to school for fundraising. I got that idea very clearly to make candy and to make it with pecans. She used raisins in hers and it was just milk and sugar. I made the pralines that Mama Tex taught me to make. Mrs. Lewis went on to become one of the first black female principals in Natchez. Miss Sadie V. Thompson was the Principal of Broomfield and the new school was named in her honor. Mrs. Lewis was also a creative and innovative teacher but in her class we also had memorable recess and that was so much fun!

On the playground there were bars and they were used a lot. We skinned the cat: we put one leg over the bar while keeping the other leg straight, tucked our head and turned over and over for several loops. The bars were very hard on the hands, but were a fun workout. There were swings on the side but they were very hard to get the chance to play on. There were basketball courts for the bigger boys and girls. Remembering the games we played reminded me of the marbles. There was always a game going on where the winner enjoyed a pocket or a sack of all the prized tiger-eye toys. This was the shooter and larger than the ordinary marble. Jacks were big but it was hard to find a smooth place to play outside. Hide and Seek games were not good because there was no place to hide. Red Light, Green Light and Mother May I? : These were just a few of the recess games we played. It was a good work out and it was fun and more fun.

I did not bike or skate at recess but I somehow learned how to do cartwheels and other tumbling stunts. I do not know how I learned to perform them. It just came natural to me. One day while doing cartwheels on the playground at recess time, a teacher on the second floor looked and called down to me. "Little girl, come up to my room #12"! I did not know who she was and knew that I was not supposed to be in the building during recess time. But when I walked around to go up the stairs, she met me and walked me around and up the stairs to her room. Her name was Miss Haynes. She wanted to know where I learned to do the tumbling stunts she saw me doing on the playground. I shared with her that I just did them and that I enjoyed doing the stunts. I kept in touch with Miss Haynes who encouraged me to improve on my skills as she looked over the playground from her second story window over the next year. Miss Haynes contributions will be more inclusive in another chapter. She definitely made an impact in my development in the physical activity area.

In order not to be the only one on campus actively turning cartwheels at recess, I taught other girls to do the stunts also. We had to wear dresses and skirts, no pants were worn by girls during this time. In order to tumble without my dress going over my head I had to tuck it in my panties legs or use a safety pin to hold it down. But it was managed. After all who wanted to show underclothes to everyone? Not me, but I could not stop tumbling, it was my niche on the playground.

Chapter 3

Ray Street and the House that our Dad Built!

While he was in school, Dad specialized in home building and concrete finishing. He knew this was just the knowledge needed in order to build the home we needed on the lot that had been purchased before we moved to Natchez. Our family made adjustments as we went to school, worked and lived on Daisy Street. We waited as dad got the house closed in from the weather and we could move in. Important steps to accomplish this meant that the foundation piers were set and leveled so that the beams could be laid on top of them. I was a process and Dad was ready for the task. In the beginning dad made a small model of the house using a half inch for each foot. We watched in amazement and anticipation as he showed us where he was in his progress at every step of the project.

Those carefully followed plans were the major steps he made to get us to the point in time so that we could move into our house on Ray Street. He put in the flooring of plain wood. Next, he framed the walls with openings for a window in every room. On the inside he put up two-by-fours to mark out the rooms so that it all fit like a jig-saw puzzle. He put the roof on the top of the building. He worked most days after he finished his shifts at the paper mill. He knew the importance of doing a little work as often as he could on our new home. He put on a front porch but not a back porch. Dad worked according to his model plan. There were no stair-steps to the front or the back doors for us to go into the house when we moved into the finished from the outside new home. Dad's goal was to complete construction of our home as soon as he possibly could. This was his goal and this is what he did. We were able to have our home even in the unfinished state it was when we moved into it. For steps there were make-shift stacks of cement blocks as a way for us to go up to and down from the doors. Those make-shift steps were adequate until my dad was able to make cement steps instead of the temporary wood steps. My dad was a lot like my Mama Tex; He learned to *make a way out of no way* as the old saying goes. This trait must have found its way to my young thinking. Later, I made things work out for my benefit in school, the community and even at home. I had the opportunity and motive to take the lead and make the choice to follow through on what my goal was.

The lot and new house were in a subdivision developed by a local land owner, Mrs. Betty White. Mrs. White was black and owned a parcel of land along North Pine Street as well as the large parcel of land behind her home which was located on North Pine Street. Mrs. White was not related to my granddad's family from White Hall Plantation. The name of the new division was Ray Street. The street had the same design as Daisy Street where my aunt and uncle lived. Ray Street was only a block long and ended at the edge of the bayou with a swamp cypress tree at the end. The reason the swamp cypress tree could grow and survive was that it was on the edge of the bayou and water ran downward towards the tree keeping it well watered every time that it rained. Fortunately, every house in the sub-division was connected to the Natchez city sewer line. No more outhouses for us. Thank God for this improvement. However, there could have been more improvements made in the subdivision to make our lives more comfortable compared to the other areas where the white citizens lived.

Why they did not put in sidewalks, so that we did not have to walk in the street was always a puzzle to me. The new subdivisions for the blacks were very different from the area that the whites lived. The black areas were not fully developed and the city did not seem to have any problem with the area. Simply stated, the *blacks lived having a lack of sidewalks.* When a new black school was built in Natchez, they put sidewalks down the lane in front of the school and cement stairs to get up the hill to the large open area in front of the school. But the lack of attention to full construction of streets and pavements was very noticeable. This was only in the black sections and it was within the city or town limits, not the county. Because of the design of the area we could ride bikes on Ray Street. There was an incline from the beginning of the street off of Pine Street. From there it slanted towards the bayou. The street was still a challenge because it had a graveled surface. However, it was a grand ride down the hill with the gravel making the challenge more risky. Thankfully, the end of the street was level, with that large swamp cypress tree as a safety area. How I got down the hill on the bike without a broken arm or leg was a remarkable feat that all the family was able to accomplish.

It was just about Halloween when we finally moved proudly into the new house. We have an established trend of making major living changes in the fall of the year. The new home got to this stage with Granddad's help. The house had finished exterior walls, a roof, rough sawn flooring and the roughed-in, one bathroom to serve the family's immediate needs. Dad put up sheets on the studs to have privacy for him and Mom, until he could put up the sheets of sheetrock. We all learned something about sheetrock, taping and mud at an early age. The floor plan was a typical one for the post war era house plan. The house was almost the same in design as the one lived in by my uncle and aunt as well as many neighbors. The back of our house did not have a porch, but theirs did. We had two front doors and two back doors. They had one front door and one back door, with a front and back porch. As we later learned, our home was to be one in transition over time.

In the beginning our home consisted of a living-room, dining room and kitchen on the right side. There was a door into a small hall just in front of the bathroom; there were closets in both of the bedrooms. We grew to love our new conveniences as they were provided. Over the next two years the rooms were finished off and painted. Furniture was brought, piece by piece. We had beds for all to sleep in the two rooms as the house was first designed. We were happy in our new home as we saw it improved from one step to the next. My mom knew that my favorite color is green and our first real living room couch and chair were both shades of green. Little by little our little house began to develop into the home that our Dad envisioned. New Organza curtains with lots of ruffles were placed in the windows with the paper roll-up shades for privacy. We had adequate lighting when the bulbs that were in every ceiling were turned on. We got a dining room table with six chairs. This was where we did our homework for school. This was where we also gathered to play checkers and board games as they became affordable. We became a very close family as we grew in our own personalities. I was excited because our family had moved into the *new middle class* subdivision for blacks. We were now experiencing, *living life* on Ray Street in Natchez, Mississippi.

The dining room was the place where all of us could be together. Food has a way of connecting people and conversations where other topics cannot. We ate breakfast and dinner together every day as a family as much as we could. Lunch during the week was at school and was affordable at twenty-five cents a week for each of us children in Vidalia and Natchez. At school, in Orange, Texas the prices were more reasonable; they always sold a little bag of raisins for a penny which was very affordable. The milk was free to all of the students and chocolate milk was my favorite. I am taking you back to let you know how the lunches compared in all three of the places when I attended school. In Orange, Texas where began my schooling I took a lunch, my choice, but it had to be just like my dad's. He had two meat sandwiches and one peanut butter and jelly sandwich. For me my mom would make two halves of the meat, and a half peanut butter and jelly. My only concern was that I had the same number of sandwiches as my dad. I had the opportunity to watch her make them and watched to make sure of what I got. I was too short and too little to help her but I had to know what kind of sandwiches we each got. The major meat was canned Spam and it was spread with mayonnaise or sandwich spread, which was my first choice. The peanut butter was always spread with apple jelly or Apple butter. I loved apple butter on a slice of white bread which we called light bread.

I remember a little girl, when I attended school in Orange, Texas whose breakfast biscuit and a piece of sausage was her lunch. She did not like for us to see what she had to eat. Light bread was expensive compared to the wonderful homemade biscuits that many families made and were sometimes left over from a previous meal. This friend was ashamed of her biscuit sandwiches. Many times, I would exchange one of my Spam, canned pressed meat sandwiches with her so that she got to eat a light bread sandwich. By sharing food and talking daily, I developed a friendship with this girl. I exchanged with her because I did not want her to feel different just because she did not have a light bread sandwich. This worked out well for both of us because we met up at lunch each day and we had a very good time. Now there were other lunch items but I did not have the five cent each day besides, I got to eat what my dad had for lunch and that was just great!

It was December of 1953 when I was twelve and living in Natchez that I realized that my friendships had grown. It was at this time that I found out more about socializing and learning about the real life in Natchez. I made friends with not only the girls in the neighborhood, but others from school also. One girl I made friends with and remember well because her mom also had lots of children. We were in the same class and they had mostly boys in their family as we had. I did not often bring people home but for some reason, with this girl I made a choice to do so. It must have been during the beginning of school or a teacher planning day.

We came to our home one day from school and found that my mom had made a pot of dried lima beans and a skillet of cornbread. Mom often left cooked food on the stove to be ready for dinner when we all got back home. My friend, whom I knew had lots of siblings, was hungry. I knew that this would take away from our relished dinner. But I dished her up some of the beans which were cooked with the ham bone that we had sliced off of from Sunday's dinner. Mom did that all of the time; she really knew how to make various meals on a tight budget. From a Picnic shoulder, which cost less than a ham, she would have a main meal on Sunday, slice off of it for sandwiches, and serve slices with the grits or oatmeal that we had for breakfast. She would always make a pot of some kind of beans on Thursday because that was the day dad got paid and she would go to town and shop for groceries.

It was strange that we could shop in the same Piggy Wiggly store with the whites and pay our money to the clerks as any other person, but we could not go into a restaurant. We also could not go through the bus station through the front entrance. There was a small area around the back with a counter in the door to the kitchen where you also had to buy your ticket. There were no restaurants downtown for blacks but there was the Savoy Grill and a soda fountain in the Dumas Drug Store which was black owned. They were both on the corner of Franklin and Pine Street. This small area was a Mecca for the *black folks.* There was also a common practice that a white customer would be waited on in a store before a black customer without any consequences if the clerk chose to do so. There was not a choice if a white came up to the counter while you were in the process of a purchase. As a black citizen you became invisible, until Miss Sally finished her transaction. There definitely was a lack of appreciation for the black consumers in the retail place during my youth. Blacks were accepting of this mentality and did not make any complaint. At the least no complaint was made at the store when the infraction was being made. During those times, it was just accepted practice. Remember that at this time whites were perceived to be *superior*.

When traveling, we had to go in the back to get bus tickets, and sit in the back of the bus. We had to buy food out of the window of the bus terminal from *coloreds* who could cook but also were not allowed to go in through the front or to ride in the bus except in the back. There were no restaurants that blacks could go into and purchase food in the downtown area, let alone sit inside to eat with the white patrons. Many of the restaurants and homes hired black cooks and yes, the whites ate the food that was cooked by the black cooks without hesitation. I could not understand the way they did things. Blacks could cook their food, while enduring their scorn and they ate it. Not a very wise decision but that's the way it was.

Aunt Carrie, who we stayed with for those months until our house was built, worked for the mayor of Natchez. She was very proud of her *position*! She cooked his food and kept his house clean. However, she had to go around to the back door to report to work. I am certain that she had the open welcome of her visitors at the back door. That was how I contacted her when I ventured there to see her or give her a message. At the very same time she would graciously open the front door and greet any white visitor with that genuine, southern hospitality. She could give it and since I knew her personality which was happy and jolly, she was a gracious greeter. I went by to see her on one particular day and as usual had to go to the back door. She walked me back around to the front when I was ready to leave. Before I left she gave me a piece of steak that had been cooked for the mayor. It was leftover from the Mayor's dinner meal. The meat was tough and chewy and not at all flavorful to my taste buds. It would not have made a good sandwich. Besides, it did not taste as good as one of my mom's fried pork chop that was usually crispy and easy to chew. Mom would have made delicious brown gravy with that dry steak smothered with lots of pungent onions, bell pepper and celery. Mom's gravy would have covered some rice, so delicious for all of us children to enjoy. She knew how to cook things like that. Mom would have served our whole family, seriously.

As I said earlier, good food is the best connector of family and activities. I learned how to cook by watching and also because by now, we had more mouths to eat my cooking experiments. My brothers loved to eat and from my recollections we ate well. We ate, lived and grew as a family as well as a neighborhood.

Ray Street had all of the lots built by now and was a close knit group of neighbors. We were all on the same telephone party line. We had different phone numbers but had to pick up on our special ring. There was expected etiquette for the phone usage. If you wanted to call and someone else was on the line already, you asked politely to use the phone. There were about three houses on one telephone line. One of our party line members was the neighborhood beautician, Mrs. Johnson who talked all day and all weekend. I know because we sometimes listened in. What, did you ask why? Well there was only so much drama on the radio. Our neighbors the Andersons would let us come over to their house on some evenings and watch their Zenith console television, which we really appreciated. No, we did not own a television but we had a nice console radio player with a turn table that played LP albums. This was before we were introduced to the popular singles which cost less and sold more to teens who could afford one every once in a while for about fifty cents. Other than that there was listening to the Radio, talking about things we imagined, wanted and were curious about in the world in which we lived.

But I had my own secret world . . . and it was reading. When I read, I learned what and how other people lived. I read about other places and neighborhoods. There were white magazines but the best magazine was the Jet which was a black publication and highlighted the life and times of the black celebrities. I read about other countries and my mom always loved traveling. I looked up as much as I could, about where people went in the publications I was able to read. Mom and I talked about the places she wanted to go and to see as I grew older. I read and I loved to read. It was my passion because I could escape the reality of segregation and expand my thinking and my mind. At the same time my mom and dad were expanding the family.

Mom discovered that she was expecting another child which would be the sixth one if it was born alive. I add this fact because Mom had several miscarriages in her earlier years. On my next birthday, I would be 13 and was starting to develop into a young lady. Prior to this time, I played with my brothers and their friends. I loved to go into the bayou and swing on the vines and forage for fruit and berries. All of those goodies grew in abundance in the tropical landscape in the middle of the adopted playground.

But just before my thirteenth birthday, I noticed a change in my body. I decided that I needed a bra and got one of my mother's bras, and modified it by stitching it to fit me. It was some crude stitching but I had the beginning skills. I carefully fitted the larger bra and continued to stitch until it was just the right fit. I never realized that my mom would find out or know what I did to her bra. In my juvenile mind, I just knew that she wore one and I had a development that needed to be covered. She talked to me about the situation and shopping together, found a bra to fit my newly developed *nipples*!

With the family growing and all of us getting older, dad had a new plan for the interior of the house. This was the second transformation he made to the house. He could not afford to change the outside dimensions so he drew up plans to change the interior. After some mathematics and dimensions were drawn to include the interior size dad made the first changes. The partition was taken out from between the living room and dining room to make it the new living-dining area. Three feet was extended into the dining room from the door to the hallway to accommodate the new closet that would serve the entire family. This opening would be in my area which was open for all to move through and get clothing from the closet. The two closets in the bedrooms were eliminated. The bedrooms were then shortened by a foot or so in order to accommodate the eight feet needed to put in my twin sized bed. The room was completed with a build-in storage and book case at the end of my bed that went across the entire width of my space. It was a space designed just for me.

My love for books started early. Reading was very important to me at a very early age. To compliment my personality and love of books, it was just natural that the bookcase, that Dad built, completed my room. The bookcase was built to store incidentals, books and would take the place of a dresser. Dad measured so that everything fit snugly in place. My room would really be complete if there was a mirror. For a vanity, which usually comes with a mirror, Mom's brother-in-law built me a neat dressing table out of recycled furniture. He made a vanity cube out of a box with a piano seat that opened for storage. There was a mirror from an old dresser that my uncle Roscoe customized. He would scavenge for project articles in New Orleans where he lived with my mother's older sister, Leanna.

Curtains for my area would enhance my revered personal space to satisfy the only girl in the family. Mom made a pink organza skirt and cover to match for my bed. A pink organza curtain for my single window completed my room. It was my princess space and I had privacy when everyone else was in their rooms. The boys stayed in their room and the baby at that time slept in a crib in my parent's room. I had my beautiful functioning space.

There in my little corner of the house I found real reading. I had access to the entire center of the house. Now, I could read in peace because I was in my own space. Have you ever read when the lights were off by a flashlight? That was my way of experiencing my passion for reading when no one else could invade my space. It was my freedom to see the world in print and visualize how I could fit into that world! I read every book I could find. There were love magazines that I should not have been reading as a part of my *literary collection*. The Natchez Democrat Newspaper was not inclusive of what I considered information. Who knew who, Mrs.

Burns' daughter and her coronation into society was all about? The best I knew of was the Elks and Masons and there were no Balls or Coronations. There was little if anything written in print about those organizations especially in the *newspaper*. So my reading material had to come from where ever I was able to find it. I did search information from family, friends and even collected the Sunday school materials. I found the library annex on Pine Street between Main and Franklin Streets. It was just a small place, but it was free and all I had to do was to sign the books out. Let me tell you a little about this little library. It was about the size of our living room at home and there was a desk in the front with shelves around the perimeter of the entire small building. The choices were limited to say the least. I do plan to share more with you about this. Reading and the library experience was to me like finding out about the limited candy store mall! But there were limited supplies and varieties to choose from which left me unsatisfied.

It was in High School in 1954 that I found out about a real library. The new school, named after the principal of Broomfield school, was Sadie V. Thompson High School. I remember my friend, Betty and I competing to see how many books we could read. When I found an author that I liked, I made it a goal to read all of their works. I was not too selective about the titles. My goal was to satisfy the hunger to know, to travel through space and time. With reading I could escape the Jim Crow life that was imposed on me, my family, my friends and everyone of color.

Remember, it was not just black or white, it was, *Colored* and *Negros*. What an infinity, colored restrooms and water fountains versus men and women restrooms and white water fountains. By the way the water was the same. It was just the titles. Just like in reading, it was not tangible, but intangible because of an attitude. The water fountains were situated side by side. I do not want to divulge what happened to some of the *white* water fountains. Some things are better not said. We read the signs with the same capacities to understand the same as we read books. But we did not always feel that segregation was something that was in our best interest. When we used the colored fountains, the water was clear. When we saw the water from the white only fountains, the water was also clear. Now who wants to argue the difference? My stand was to keep reading because somewhere and in some other lives, segregation was the rule not the exception. The chance to read more and have a better selection for me was now like the unlimited candy store mall. There were more choices and varieties of books for everyone who wanted or needed them.

Reading enlightened me to other choices and ideas. I now had a greater perception of the world in which I lived. I saw that my living could be better and even more than what my experiences were at that time. I read about the trains and the highways that cut thought the Rocky Mountains. I read about other countries and how the people enjoyed living in harmony regardless of their ethnicity. I read the Chicago Defender and understood why so many blacks left Mississippi to migrate to the north. I read how jobs and housing were available to the masses and that it was not just your the state of mind to be denied this normal lifestyle. It was believed that you had to live life as a second class citizen which was the norm in my loving state of Mississippi. I read myself into an elevated self appreciation for who I was. I learned what others in other places experienced as a reality that my family was denied just because of whom and where we lived. I read how I could be respected as an individual. I read how life could be better if not but by the state of mind. In reality, I read that life was not the same as my daily experiences. No wonder I loved to read so much. This love for reading has continued for the span of my life and culminated in a library of my own. Because of my ongoing love of reading, I made my second investment in books.

When I got my first job as a full time teacher, I purchased the entire, Writers of the Western World. It was like a great investment into not only the future but the classics of, from where we came. This was the pattern that I wanted to pursue for my lifetime. I credit reading as one of my best attributes to the quest for higher learning and living. My investment in the great writers was a gift to myself.

Part 2:
Learning through Development: Educationally, Emotionally and Physically!

Chapter 4

My Birthday Present and other Gifts!

By the time I was anticipating my thirteenth birthday and planning to have a birthday party to celebrate, Mom went into labor. Now what happened put my plans for my first birthday party at risk. It seemed I would not be getting my anticipated gift to acknowledging my first teen year. Mom had other plans and had the baby boy a day before my birthday. Here we go with the short word, I! There may be a better word to use but my feeling is that the disappointment was enough. I did grow educationally, but at the time of my remembrances of this time and occasion, it was all about me for a change. So if you do not understand why the word for me is used so much, just put yourself in my emotional state and change the word or rather the letter to suit your correct usage. This was a very strong emotional part of my life to digest. However, it is only ground one for what is yet to come. I was disappointed! No, I was disappointed, hurt and probably angry that the new baby was messing up my planned party. After everything happened, in the end with the timing of the birth I got the opportunity for both emotional and physical growth. Because my mom could not be there it forced me to take action. I had to continue to grow up and found myself in a place few young adults may have found themselves in. But I took it all in stride. After all, I had seen the results of all of my last brothers. I remembered the births and not only the births but the fact that every time, it was another boy. The first one was not one that I remembered because I was very young at the time. Every time a new brother was born, I always felt letdown. I wanted a little sister with each new birth. This was no different, except for the fact that I was forced to take charge and put my own plans into action.

My baby brother and I stated out with a special bond. As I reflect, I realized that he really was a birthday present. Afterwards, I always referred to him as my birthday present. I got the honor of naming my baby brother. By that time in my life, I was checking out the cute boys in school. There was this really popular one whose name was Lawrence. So we all decided on my brother's name being David. My contribution was to give him the middle name of "Lawrence". Whenever, I say his name it's in a loving way because I use both names even to this day. He was not just David but David Lawrence!

My brother David was the one who caused me to gather up my emotions and become self confident. With the setback of not having my mom to depend on, I learned what I now know as self-assurance. There was definitely some development from this occasion.

I had a set-back in my birthday plan because it did not include a new baby brother. Mom was in the hospital I had to set up a new plan. To succeed I had to put into action a comeback plan. My birthday is in the summer and invitations were already given out before school was out. All of the classmates and friends were given the information before school was out. Many whose phone number and addresses I probably did not know were looking forward to attending. During those years, we did not have the social interaction tools that are available in the twenty-first century. We were just into telephones with the revered single line for all who could afford them. After the shock and disappointment of mom not being able to be there, my formulated plan was to make it all happen to have my thirteenth birthday party. Someone was going to have to do the work since she was in the hospital. They kept you in the hospital for three days when you delivered a baby. Dad was there at the hospital when he was not at work.

I had worked to do on my checklist. Now, I just had to put it all together. Invitations had been given out, ingredients were on hand for homemade cake and ice cream, and the party was still on. I could make it happen. I was looking forward to my friends and classmates coming to enjoy my party with me. The task had to be done.

Decisions were always being made by me because I was the oldest child. My grandmother Texanna was there with us but I had to do the work. Cooking was something I enjoyed. Taking Homemaking as a class in school was my choice whenever I had the opportunity. I often made cornbread from a recipe. I had started to make Pralines weekly to sell at school. Money made from Pralines was used to buy things I needed for myself. I had to be creative and focused to get the things that I needed and wanted. Money was not something that we were accustomed to getting, but I wanted to do the little things I needed to do. This desire for self—sufficiency as I later learned was the term, was what motivated me to do some of the things I learned to do in order to make money for myself. There were not any babysitting jobs to be had, because every family had built-in family care. I was too young for a job and I wanted to make things happen for myself. Having this mindset, I decided to be my own chef, cook and hostess for my thirteenth birthday party. Plans for my party to go on as planned were in place. From my thirteenth birthday party experiences I learned early to make plans and to follow through on them.

My party was very important to me. I really wanted my 13th birthday party to be a success. My Mother could not be there to make the food and get it ready for me, so I enlisted my dad to get ice and coarse salt for the ice cream. I was familiar with being in the kitchen and I knew how to read the recipes. I was highly motivated to cook for this party and I also knew what needed to be cooked. There was nothing to keep me from making the foods that were needed. My experiences made me familiar with making cornbread, brownies with pecans that I shelled, and with corn popped on top of the stove in a heavy metal pot. This was the only way to pop corn. No air poppers and, as my granddaughter would lament, "no microwave?"

Making the food and desserts was not going to be no problem. I prepared myself and as I read the recipes, made the custard for the ice cream and cooled it down. I baked the cake in layers and stacked them successfully. My favorite color is green. Without any hesitation I chose to use green food coloring for the ice cream and the icing on the cake. This is what I did and we had green cake and ice cream. There were tuna sandwiches, made and cut in rectangles for a good presentation. Ritz crackers were covered in baloney and cheddar cheese and topped with a little red pimento. I had everything, including the music and decorations, ready by party time! At the appropriate time, I cleaned myself up, put on my prettiest outfit which was also a hue of green and gave my full lips their first application of some of my mom's lipstick. I was thirteen and had proven myself to be a young lady.

Neighbors told me afterwards how I impressed them with my successful birthday party. The Andersons teased me because I wore lipstick. I was not going to soon forget this demonstration of physical and emotional growth. Everything was cohesive as everyone worked together to see that my thirteenth birthday party was a success especially, with my mom being in the hospital. I had a special role in my first teenage birthday party being successfully! I had the help of the Andersons who were the only family on Ray Street to have a carport at the time. I was given their consent and blessings to have my party in their carport with our phonograph and LP Records. Their carport was located between our houses, making it really handy. We were all set with all of the foods and some new and borrowed LP's. We waited for dusk to see the boys and girls arrive and the dancing begins.

By the way, dancing was also one of my passions along with reading, which we talked about earlier. In fact, dancing was one of my first self expressions. As far back as I could remember once we moved back to Vidalia my Aunt Lucille had a business that encouraged the youngsters to dance. There was always a jukebox in the small business which was in the front part of her home. There was no problem getting the youngsters and teens to put their nickels and quarters in the Jukebox to have the opportunity to dance and just listen as recreation. Dancing was called, "cutting a gig" by the older population. Dancing was one of our best recreational activities. Teenagers loved home parties and the opportunity to dance or just to socialize and watch others dance. But then, what else was there to do on a warm sultry summer night for youngsters who were just experiencing the hormonal changes that come without any encouragement when you turn thirteen? Every year, from that time on I threw the best summer time *party* in the neighborhood. *Everyone looked forward to my Birthday parties!*

Although we were healthy, active, and impressionable there was something else in the mix. We did not completely understand it but we were being prepared for young adulthood in more that the physical realm. We had to deal with life in the physical and biological sense anticipating all that we would later become. With physical development came responsibility, commitment, and dependability. Those were just a few of the traits and characteristics we would learn as we progressed from year to year. We would have to address varying attitudes that developed as we grew. We had to combine the carefree nature with the new things learned that all youth experience. We also had to try to maneuver the very rollercoaster of emotions that our bodies took us through. Wow, what a time of physical and emotional loops we had to encounter. I look back and think, what a wonderful time to have lived in, for those years of physical and emotional growth. They were a challenge then but the support system was so very nurturing from family, extended family and neighbors. We lived in a segregated society yet it was safe. We had community support and intervention with neighbors, extended family and ideals that are no longer a part of the *black* experience. However, I am happy that it took place when it did. At the tender age of thirteen, there was the once in a lifetime process of the body developing into a form that has never been before. At the same time of physical growth spurts we had to live with a mind that still wanted to play the innocent games that have been parts of everyday life. As a result we had the life expectations of increasing the personal level of responsibility that comes with being a *teenager* or young adult. Now, I can share that with my granddaughter and her children. I have been in that stage and was empowered to move forward as in individual.

I thank God for that time and place of my life. The neighbors were watchful of all of our actions. They showed concern for the way I dressed and could tell me what outfits of clothing I wore from day to day. Many of their concerns seemed to be just plain nosey. However, I was respectful and politely acknowledged their observations. This was especially true for my hairdresser, because she not only noticed but shared her observations with all of her clients, which included my mother. There was one who was also the mother of my classmate and friend in the Ray Street neighborhood who spotted that I did not have on a half-slip on one hot day. After a face to face talk she called my attention to this very important dress code. She bought me indoors and gave me one of my friend's half-slips to wear, because that was the appropriate way to dress. This act on mom's intervention was out of love and was received by me as a loving gesture.

I enjoyed dressing in the outfits that I designed and sewed when I learned how to sew with my mom's help. In the summer while they were fashionable I would make myself a full skirt. It consisted of gathering three yards of material and making a band of 24 inches to fit my 22 inch waistline. I used the remainder of the material from the bottom to make a sash to further cinch my waistline. There was always a hem at the bottom to finish the garment. It took all of the three yards of material to get the fullness needed to wear over my cancan starched bouffant slip. I made a new skirt as often as I got the money and found the special pattern or color I wanted. My brothers always wanted me to make them a shirt. However, blouses and shirts were not my strong items. For blouses I made some off the shoulder tops but I enjoyed buying my colorful, cardigan sweater sets. After the simmering summers of the humid Mississippi area with its infestation of mosquitoes, I looked forward to each fall season.

I enjoyed the four seasons that we had in the Mississippi climate. But the fall of the year was the best because it began a new year of school and new challenges. Soon, I became 14, 15, 16, and 17. Each year had offerings of continued growth and development to get me to my goals with my parents' expectations. I was a typical girl of the '50's. I dated and danced and enjoyed the leisure that was made available to *us*. That was the colored teenagers.

Summers, once I was in high school found me as an assistant to Miss Haynes, for table tennis, badminton and other individual sports. The chapter devoted to this dear teacher will tell you more on how she mentored me as I grew, developed and became a potential young college student. I enjoyed this opportunity as an assistant for social interaction. Summers were long, afternoons hot and humid. The sun and heat, found me and many others at the local swimming pool. This segregated public pool was situated midway between the Sadie V. Thompson School (SVT) and the Historical Natchez College.

I remember, one summer that all of my brothers and I were in the pool and they all swam like little fish. We all would dive off of the side of the pool. Being who I am, I went to the low diving board and dove in. Afterwards all of my brothers followed and also used the low diving board. I had no lessons or experience but, eventually had the audacity to do a Swan dive from the high diving board. This started a new challenge for Pete, John, Ezell, and Noel. David was too young to go from the diving boards and played duck and dive in the four feet section, but was a good swimmer. I really enjoyed the interactive relationship my brothers and I had. I was the oldest and if I was going to set the bar of participation, I felt that I had to be first!

I remember being very interested in the gymnasium and all that it had to offer. I remember the smell of the gym and the unused shower part of the dressing room. There was the smell of running shoes and sweating that lingered long past its due time. This need for cleanliness and being an athlete at the same time would later be stressed as an important attribute from me. As a teacher of Physical Education much later, cleanliness was stressed as an all important part of being healthy, fit and well! We were required to dress but there was no showering. It was a musty place. The dressing room was just that, a convient place to put on the gym clothes and suit up for a game of the current sport.

Many families did not shower nor had showers as a part of the bath experience, so showers were not the norm in the late 1950's when I was in high school. Bathing in the wonderful ceramic bath tubs with hot and cold water was the hygiene of those times. The shower room of the gym experience was not fully utilized, not for lack of good hygiene but because the idea of open shower areas were not normal for an individual let alone in a group.

It was almost a luxury to have a full functioning bathroom for many black citizens during those years. The use of the #3 which was a galvanized round tub used both for washing clothes as well as bathing was a part of most households. The #2 was a foot-tub that was also used. Both were used in our Vidalia family home during the '40s and were not a problem. This tidbit was bought up because you may not be aware of this method of personal hygiene that my family used until we moved to Natchez in 1950.

I remember the auditorium and the dressing room to the left facing the stage. It was where I kept my shorts to practice my dance and acrobatic acts that I performed at every opportunity. We did have a large football field and area for the marching band to practice on. I was right there in the mix. I was a majorette and played as many of the sports as they had for the girls. I took pride in always being healthy and fit. I soon developed my tumbling skills into a rare acrobatic act which I improved on each year with bolder and more daring moves. My talents were very much rooted in Physical Activities and Dance. I learned a lot during my developing teen years about the physical, emotional and educational parts of life.

In school I took courses every class period that I could. Study hall was not something that I wanted to use my time for. I had to go there sometimes, but my schedule was filled with classes of electives. I took the homemaking as an elective every semester. I took physical education all four years. I sang in the school chorus and was a majorette with the marching band. I played softball and basketball. I ran track and participated in the field events. Math was a subject that I was turned on to in the fourth grade when I competed to get the answers first. To me in the fourth grade the quest to solve the problems were like making a score in a ball game. It was for the attention and the more I got the answers correct, and held up my hand, the more recognition I received. I remember the teacher also changing the method of problem solving to the paper work and we had to wait to see what points we received. This was less challenging but Mom and Dad expected me to do my best. In the ninth grade, I had an unfortunate experience with the male teacher and ended up getting a failing grade. The next term after enrolling back into the same class, he warned me that I would get the same grade if I did not decide to do what he wanted me to do. I boldly stated to him in return that He could not fail me because I was going to be the best student in the class. I took all of the mathematic classes that were offered for the remainder of my high school days. I really enjoyed my mathematic challenges.

As a freshman, I was invited to the Junior/Senior prom and I had no problem in securing this very prestigious date. I was invited when I was a sophomore, again with a senior. I became a junior and went alone because I did not have to be invited, I could dance regardless. By the time I was a senior, the Prom had lost its glamour. But glamorous I was, because I had two Prom gowns to choose from. My aunts and Uncle Roscoe each bought me an outfit when something major was happening. Both aunts and my mother were seamstresses and could make any item that I chose to have for any of the ceremonies that I was in. For the Senior Prom my uncle bought me two or three beautiful prom dresses to choose from and I chose to have my dad drive me and come back for me. My fun was in the dancing and I was one of the girls that stayed on the floor because, dancing is what I did best! My desire was to excel on the dance floor no matter the ability of my dance partner. My partners were few and they could dance too!

I connected with a girl who was also serious about education and forged a strong friendship with her. Our junior and senior years were ripe with hormones and jockeying for the attention of the football and other athletic stars' attention. I chose to focus and forge towards my goal of excellence in my grades. Do not get me wrong, I was in the mix but I held the card of confidence and it was on my terms for any *boyfriend*. My friend, whose name was Betty, turned out to be a very serious student. She was the best inspiration for me to balance my active mind and body and challenge myself in the intellectual arena. She became the Salutatory and I was fifth in the class of 105 students the class of '59. That dang F grade I got in my freshman Algebra class came back to kick me in the butt. I should have protested at that time and I had a good cause.

That teacher propositioned me and I resisted. I had repeated the Algebra class and made an A. The instructor was wrong and it had made me more determined to succeed in his class the next year. No malice was held in my heart for what he did. But, I made it up when I returned one year after receiving my first Masters Degree. I addressed him by his first name, because he was always adamant about being addressed by his professional name. My husband was with me and I introduced him and with a twinkle in my eye, I let my former teacher know that his disservice to me as a girl did not deter me from accomplishing my goals in life. In fact, Mathematics was and still is one of my strong subjects.

I graduated from High-School in May of 1959 without any further incidents. With the help of our counselor and senior sponsors, which included Miss Haynes, I found myself striving to be a student at Tougaloo Southern Christian, College in Tougaloo, Mississippi, just north of Jackson, Mississippi.

Chapter 5

Miss Haynes, a Favorite Teacher!

My mentor, a long time sponsor of the senior class and homeroom teacher, was dearly loved and respected by the seniors and graduates in Natchez, Mississippi. She was lovingly called not just by her name but also, *Dear Teacher*!

This all started at Broomfield School which went from first to twelfth grades. Later, the new Sadie V. Thompson High School (SVT) was built in time to have its first class to graduate in 1954. The classes covered the grades seventh to twelfth. Broomfield became an Elementary School grades first through sixth. Prince Street Elementary School was in the area where I lived and it housed first through third grades.

I was in the fifth grade when I started attending Broomfield on the south-east side of Natchez. It was the only school for the black students because of the limited grades available in our area. Now, that you understand why I went to Broomfield school, let me introduce you to how I came to know Miss Haynes. I was playing at recess when she spotted me on the Playground. One day from her classroom on the second floor of the school building, Miss Haynes looked down and called to me. "Little girl", she said, "come up to my room # 12 on the second floor". I then had *fear*.

What had I done and why did she want to see me? She did not call the other girls with whom I was playing. I did not realize it at the time but Miss Haynes had been observing me for a long time.

It was not permissible to be on the second floor but she met me and walked me to her room. She introduced herself to me and asked me my name. She wanted to know where I learned to do the *stunts* she saw me doing. I could not tell her where or how, because I had been doing them as long as I could remember. I do not remember seeing them done. It just felt right to do them and they were fun. I could, I would and I did. I used any vacant wall at home to do a handstand against. Headstands, handstands and more as my skills improved. I was moved to do more and more. As far back as I can remember I was physically active in everything I had an opportunity to be. No television, radio or books described the things that came natural to me.

The sixth grade at Broomfield School went by with my memories of a teacher who taught from her desk. There was no interaction with her. I do not even remember her name. However, the next year the new school was ready and so was I. When we moved to the new school, (SVT) I was in the seventh grade. Physical Education was not given to the seventh grade class because we were in the south wing and had recess. There was no distinction such as Junior High or even Middle School at that time. The entire school was known as SVT High School. I do believe that the classes were from grades fourth to eighth in the south wing. The Prince Street School continued to offer classes only to the third grade.

Miss Haynes sent for me at our recess time and anytime she could get me out of class. She taught me things she learned during the summer when she attended the Texas Women's College. She let me demonstrate the skills she taught me to her classes of ninth to twelfth graders.

When I began ninth grade, I had Physical Education. Miss Haynes let me lead exercises, and continue to demonstrate skills for the other students. She showed me books on activities and I was all eyes. I learned a lot from Miss Haynes.

During the summer she did the recreation for the black students. I shared earlier some of the individual skills that I was able to learn and participate in because of this summer recreation program. There was only one site for recreation in the entire town for blacks. This site only utilized a short wing on the elementary side of the SVT School. Miss Haynes had a short hallway, the restrooms and a room for office and storage space for her program each summer. She could not hire anyone because they only provided for one paid leader. Miss Haynes let me volunteer every day. I learned how to set up equipment the proper care of the small equipment and how to play games I previously had no clue about. This is when I really was able to learn and play individual sports and board games. It was a lot of fun and it was an exciting time for me. Miss Haynes would give me a couple of dollars a week to encourage me. Although, she made very little, she was generous enough to share with me each summer. At summers' end I had enough from the summer to buy the material to make all of my skirts and buy a couple of sweaters.

No pants were worn during those years. So, I made my own wardrobe of stylish short shorts with my mom's, and aunts' help. We ended up sewing quite a lot of outfits during the summer months. I wore shorts all summer because of the recreational games and sports. Shorts were the outfit to wear in the hot and humid Mississippi Summers. I was comfortable in my summer attire. I was assured and confident because I always learned something that I could share. The other students benefited by my gained skills and so did my brothers. I learned leadership skills without really trying to. I just did what was needed to be done and if someone wanted to go where I was going, they naturally, had to follow. What is the definition of a leader? At that time, I did not know or probably even cared. I was involved, motivated and satisfied to be able to play the games and understand the rules. I could learn; have goals to accomplish as many of the skills and objectives that were attainable and sometimes teachable.

PART 3:
TOUGALOO COLLEGE

Chapter 6

Making the transformation from High School

While in high school, had there been such an acknowledgement for, *Top Physical Education Student,* it would have been me. You do not have to agree with me because of what I experienced and the years that I devoted to this activity makes me certain of that fact. I was on a fast track to achieve this acknowledgment. Though, that was never my goal. The fact is that I really enjoyed being active from as far back as I can remember. The only reason I did not participate in some of the games and activities was that I did not know about them. I learned over time that what I loved to do was to play and I enjoyed all that was introduced to me. I soon learned that this love of activities had a specific title.

Physical Education and Physical Activities were a passion along with dance. I was physically active with a purpose. It was a long time before I knew what the subject was but that did not keep me from doing all of the things that I felt comfortable doing. There was no activity that I tried out for that I did not make the team or performance. I knew my limitations because my mom taught me to sing a song and it was not something that I felt comfortable doing. Both mom and dad were singers. I was not a singer but I had no fear of failure in any physical activity. I had no fear of living in the fast lane or speeding to the next level in running, jumping or even playing sand lot ball.

I personally feel that I was handicapped by the school district that I was a part of, because of the *Separate but Equal Education System*. Not just in curriculum but in the opportunity to demonstrate what I could do, because it was not taught. Gymnastics was one of those things that I did not have a clue about although I did all of the skills even to swinging on the bars of the playground structures. Dance Education was another course not because of my teacher but because it was not taught in school or given to me when I could have had the opportunity. Do not get me wrong our teachers were great and I remember so many of them from then, even to this day. We were excited about our school and we were serious about our studies. I learned that there was much to be disappointed about the courses offer and opportunities to learn.

Miss Haynes introduced me to a dance studio on Commerce Street but I was not able to attend because of my race, not my ability. The white dance teacher was gracious and let me tour the facility with Miss Haynes but rejected me as a student. To pacify me they gave me a used pair of ballet slippers and I graciously accepted them. This was just one of many rejections I experienced. Miss Haynes tried to assist me in getting the courses that would have helped in her area of teaching. In the other curriculum issues, there were situations that were disappointing not only to me but to the entire student body.

We were disappointed when we were told that we would get new text books only to find that we actually received the cast-offs from the white school. This told us that we were not equal. This let us know that we were perceived as not worthy of having the same educational materials at the same time as the whites. This was the open degradation shown to us during my entire school days at the brand new high school.

The superintendent, whose name I remember better than those of some of the teachers, was deeply set in my memory even before I learned that the elementary school on Highway 61 was renamed in his honor. I felt that his friendly face and demeanor were not in our best interest. His smile was always there as he represented the superintendent's office when he came to events at our school. He did not give us the materials and support that would have justified, *separate but equal* treatments. This injustice was demonstrated emphatically by the old text books and other materials sent to us at SVT from 1954 to 1959 while I attended there. I remember getting new to us textbooks, only to have all of the spaces for names already filled in. This is how the superintendant treated the black students equally in educational materials. This reality let me know what I had to overcome in learning to live and make my educational decisions in the future. When we started our education with the used texts, we were five years behind in that part of our education. I do not remember how many of the years this caper was pulled on our fellow students. But I knew that it was not right. What do you think?

I did not know anything about finishing school early when I was enrolled at Sadie V. Thompson. I took every class I could and finished with 21 units. I only needed 18 units to graduate. Even in high school, I was determined to do my best and maximize my abilities to learn and achieve.

I was not perfect while in high school. My one regret then, was that I did not realize my potential at an earlier age. As an example, I had an attitude problem in Algebra during the ninth grade. Rather than sharing the incident with the administration or my parents, I chose to cut classes or go somewhere else. I had to repeat Algebra the next year as I shared earlier.

Mathematics turned out to be a subject that challenged me to be on top of learning the equation and information rather than the recognition of being first to solve a problem. With this realization Mathematics became a subject I really enjoyed. Having to repeat an Algebra class was realized as a waste of my time. The administration and my parents could have resolved the conflict. Soon, I began to realize that I liked to be successful and thrived on an educational challenge.

Reading was a passion for me as was Physical Education. When we moved to the brand new school on the northwest side of town, closer to home, I was delighted. The year was 1954 and it was after the summer I turned thirteen. That's another chapter that you already know about. What I discovered at the beginning of the school year was the brand new and unknown to me, Library at Sadie V. Thompson High School. Before this library, Natchez's only library for the *Colored* was an auxiliary library, downtown on Pine Street between Main and Franklin Streets. There was a public library on Commerce Street or in that area. We could not go into this public library and they made a *separate but equal* place for the colored citizens. The place must have been all of 12x12 feet in size. It was also limited in titles. But I frequented it often once I found out that I could check out books and it was free.

The new library at Sadie V. Thompson had the Dewey decimal system which I quickly learned. I also learned to follow the titles of certain writers until I read all of their works. The big deal in those first years was the United Nations. I read everything I could get my hands on about this organization.

My appetite for reading was insatiable. My privacy at home was limited, while my desire to read was unlimited. I read with a flash light under the covers of my bed at night so that my parents could not know. They always asked me to turn off the light and go to bed but I found a way around this. My reading was a direct inspiration for the desire to attend college.

To make my transition from high school to college took much intervention from parents, family and teachers. Although, I shared with you what Miss Haynes contributed to me as a girl, she had a hand in more, especially about college. She served me as a mentor by just taking interest and sharing tidbits of her growth in higher learning requirements. She had to go to college every other summer to keep her teaching credential current. When she returned, she did not give me details on entrance, classes or other relevant information. What she did share was her new information, which she shared liberally. She shared her inspiration and I got the excitement for learning on the college level.

Miss Haynes would introduce me to new dances. For example, the *Glow Worm* was a folk dance that she introduced me to and we worked out the steps to demonstrate to the classes. I knew that she went to Texas Women's College in Texarkana, Texas. She talked about many of her experiences in the activity classes and really got my attention. From Miss Haynes sharing, I had some visual insight to college before I went on my freshman orientation tour of Tougaloo Southern Christian College Campus.

Chapter 7

Finances and Making it Through Tougaloo College

When I think of how I got through Tougaloo College, It was a true blessing from God. I had my dedicated parents and their total support. I had a mentor in the Physical Education Major who programmed my schedule of classes for me to follow. My friend from high school gave me a favorable educational partnership. She too, was a player in my educational game plan, because she was a serious student. I salute her because she was an excellent education partner. If you want to accomplish anything in life, as I did as a young adult, you need to surround yourself with people who think the same way. My friend was a highly motivated student and a true survivor. Unlike me she did not have a strong support system. Her mom was deceased and she lived with an older sister and her five kids. This arrangement left little time for nurturing and most of all no financial support. Thankfully, she had the opportunity to attend school and successfully finish high school with a desire to further her education. I recognized this characteristic in her before our high school senior year. She was also interested in attending Tougaloo College in Tougaloo Mississippi. I admired her strong desire to make it in spite of the obstacles in her life. My friend had a strong determination to succeed in life. It was satisfying being friends because of her thinking. She was as challenging as a game of my favorite sports. To make sure she got the opportunity to enroll in Tougaloo College, I asked my parents if she could go along with us. My parents would serve as advocates for her. Mom and Dad carried her along with us to the orientation to Tougaloo College in the summer of 1959. Being the caring individuals they were it posed no problems for them. They walked us both through the registration. My friend was able to get a larger scholarship than I but we both signed up for work study and college loans.

The school session, beginning in the fall of 1959, found me in possession of my partial scholarship. The orientation during the summer let my parents know that in addition to the small scholarship from the college, there was a small student financial loan to be paid back to the Federal Government when I started to work. I would have to be responsible for only half of the loan if I chose teaching as a career. That was just what my plans were. In addition there was the contract to do work-study to help support a portion of my college expenses. After my parents figured out what was owed they sacrificed and agreed to pay the needed $100.00 each month for the remainder of my college expenses. I calculated this amount for three years and including the summer sessions knew that my parents had committed to the sum of $3,600.00. If I chose to go to school for the four years, $4,800.00 would be needed for my college expenses. This did not include individual travel, clothing and etc. Dad made $100.00 a week at the time. I had a brother who was three years behind me in high school. My calculations were that if I could finish Tougaloo College in three years, my family would be relieved of some of the expenses and be able to help my brother to attend college. I knew that to have both of us in college for even an overlap of one year would be impossible. I also knew that I was blessed to have a small scholarship and could have continued work-study. My brother only had sports as a possibility to assist him. So my financial awareness was jump started as I figured out what was best for the family, not just for me. Finances are a subject that is so very important for your lifespan. I credit my college years as a tried and true test on how to acquire, manage and spend whatever amount of money I had. When I attended Tougaloo College, all meals were included, except for my third summer. The work-study helped to keep the fees down and my personal ability to acquire pocket change was an asset. My parents did not have the money for anything other than the necessities. There were five boys still at home and my mom was basically a housewife. She did not earn a salary nor did she work a steady job. She sold a little Avon as well as worked at the small family business which was not a high earning venue. The values that I learned prior to attending Tougaloo were definitely instrumental in giving me the ability to make it on what I had.

Fast forwarding for a moment, in order to make it in college as I did, I have to acknowledge that I was truly blessed. I knew my strengths to work things out in my favor. One big expense in college was getting back and forth to school on Holidays. Travel turned out to be no real problem to and from my home in Natchez, thanks to the generosity of the West Family. George was a student from Natchez and a year ahead of me at Tougaloo. His parents owned the major Funeral Home in Natchez. During those years the West family offered me the opportunity to travel along in a car that they sent each Holiday for their son.

As I stated before, my extended family helped according to their financial ability. I was the very first to attend college on both my mom's and dad's side of the families. Both families were proud of me and tried to show their support. They were supportive in the basic necessities!

When I look back on the time and what I had to work with, I know that I was blessed and that I learned how to do what Mama Tex, always stressed. She taught me to make do with the resources that I had to work with. Again, I am blessed to have learned this awesome financial lesson very early in my life.

The elective classes that I took while in high school turned out to be well worth the time and solidified my understanding of home and personal finances. The best lesson I learned in order to support my clothing needs was the sewing classes I had earlier while in high school. My second year in sewing class at SVT, I made a green suit with a white collar. Purchasing the material and making that suit was a great comparison of cost and savings to a similar one in the retail store from which I got the idea and made my own design. By designing and making that suit out of similar materials the cost was about 25% of the one in the store. This example showed that I could support my clothing expenses while in college. I learned to sew and to be somewhat fashionable. The outfit being described was fitted with a fish tail bottom. It looked like something any model would wear and yours truly was on a new roll. Sewing became a new passion as well as a financial benefit, which assured that I was always dressed fashionably for all occasions. You may wonder how college and sewing is connected. Well, money connects all of these variables. The 1950's were unlike the times now, there were no credit cards and you had to buy what you needed and paid for it, with cash. That is why sewing was ultimately so important in college. I am grateful, that I learned to sew in the years I spent in Home Economics while in high school. I sewed my own clothes mostly during the vacation time away from college. Since I could sew whatever I needed, there was only the need to acquire materials, which my aunts were very generous with. This was a great source of family support during my years at Tougaloo.

My sundry items were supplied by my aunt, Leanna and her husband, Roscoe. My aunt, Lucille supplied my canned goods that I carried to college in one of my Samsonite suitcases from her store in Ferriday, Louisiana whenever I came home. The Samsonite luggage set was a graduation gift to me from my parents. This sturdy luggage was a part of my good support system because of its durability.

My mom would send me a box of goodies in the mail every month or so. For those long stretches between holidays, it was a joy to receive something from home to go along with those weekly letters of assurance, written in green ink from my mother. All I had to do was to be serious about my studies and to reach my goal, to finish in three years and three summers.

For expenses incurred I had to use ingenuity to stay afloat. Managing what I got from family and friends for graduation presents the first year went a long way. While in high school my hair was done by a neighbor who had a beauty shop in her home. When I went to Tougaloo, I quickly learned to do my own hair. I experimented on others and soon found myself, *frying hair*, which was the term I used for pressing hair. I was not very experienced in this skill; so for financial support, I only charged up to 50 cents a head. I averaged about $1.50 per week. It was just enough for my sundry and personal hygiene needs. I was a typical college student and had the insight to believe in the possibility of, *I can*! My work-study was to clean the hallways of our dorm. This was done along with my friend from S.V.T. High School every night during our freshman and a portion of the second year. We usually did this work around mid-night after the resident students were in bed. My friend and I would put on our pajamas and get out the large mops from the custodians closet and run up and down the hall ways as fast as we could. Our job was to clean the hallways of the dormitory. That was our task and that is what we did. The sooner we finished, the sooner we could go to sleep. She was a hard working young lady. We were roommates for both freshman and my second year at Tougaloo. Because I went to school both summers, I was a senior my third year and did my student teaching course work and field work in the summer of '62. My graduating class was '63 but I was not a part of it. This too is why my story is something that I want you to know. I was successful and met my goals but only because I was on a fast track. My friend was also successful in her work ethics both financially and educationally and was a graduate of the class of '63.

I want you to continue to virtually walk with me as I share the three years and three summers' journey I experienced on the Tougaloo College campus.

Chapter 8

Tougaloo College Campus Experiences

On my tour of the Tougaloo College campus the summer before classes began, my guide was an upper-class Physical Education major. He was also from the American Panama Canal Zone and stayed in the United States for the entire time he attended Tougaloo College. He shared with me how he had scheduled his classes to finish his course work in three years. I was very interested in how he did this. My major was to be Physical Education. When I shared my desire to also finish in three years, he responded by getting a class schedule booklet and notating what to do and when. I was on the path to getting my goals in progress.

When I came to Tougaloo College in the summer of 1959, I was impressed. I did have limited knowledge of college through the small Natchez College adjacent to my High School. There was never any thoughts of attending Natchez College, although it was a community college rich in history all its own. In addition to being a Community College, it served as a high school campus for all of the *Negro* students who lived in the County. It was probably for this reason I did not consider Natchez for the excellent College that it was. *Natchez College also housed an early childhood program. My mother was a very active and supportive parent in all of the schools and educational settings affecting her children.* My baby brother David was enrolled there when she was a volunteer. The pre-school at Natchez College was one of the reasons I knew as much as I did about the college.

Natchez College was the setting for a fashion show produced by aspiring fashion and homemaking students. My entry was one I remember very well. It was very unusual at the time and was characteristic of my favorite color, green. It was a body molded strapped sheik dress. It had a ruffled tie-around that could be worn at the waist or used to cover the shoulders. It was designed to be worn for multiple occasions day and night. It was one of my own designs. I was an aspiring designer for my own wardrobe using independent creative thinking. My designs were often the results of the type and amount of material I had to work with. Once I learned to sew, I designed and made all of my clothing for many years.

My experience in high school was a good experience in studying and maximizing my class work. I had no problems carrying a full load of classes and leading a very active social, family and church attendance life. Coming from a large family and being the oldest prepared me both for responsibility and sacrifice at the same time. If I had any doubts or apprehensions about Tougaloo Christian College, they were all resolved when I first stepped on the campus. There were lots of majestic oak and fragrant magnolia trees all over the campus. There were dormitories and a grand mansion that was used for the president's resident. There was a library that was open in the evenings. There was a canteen under my soon-to-be dormitory and small businesses just outside of the stately gate to the campus. During these years the city of

Jackson was some miles to the south. There were open fields and open areas all over campus. You could walk for long distances in solitude and still be on the school's property. The sidewalks that crisscrossed the campus were like a maze. Sidewalks come back to my memory because there were so few when I was growing up in Vidalia and Natchez. There were none in the neighborhoods where we, the black citizens lived. On campus you just had to head in the right direction traveling on one sidewalk or another. You walked at your own pace or faster to beat the crowd to your desired destination. The mazes of sidewalks were beautiful. The sidewalk mazes were an opportunity to see the beauty of the serene campus; and to carry you to the places to learn the subject matter that was offered in the Liberal Arts buildings on campus. The major emphasis of the college was to know that when you left that place of academia you would be equipped to lead in all areas of your major and/or minor studies.

It did get a little confusing with my schedule even for me at times because I could not tell you what my status was as a student. I took my freshman classes, and then during my first summer, I took my junior subjects and some of my sophomore classes. My second year came in with me still in Judson Hall for young women and taking sophomore and more junior classes. During my second year, Dean Branch called me into the office and asked me, "Why do you not like it at Tougaloo?" I assured him that I did like being at Tougaloo. He then asked me, "Why are you trying to get out of Tougaloo so fast?" At the time he called for me to come into his office, I was carrying twenty one units of classes. He let me go with his wise advice. He essentially told me to take it easier and enjoy my education. He did not know it but I was having a great time at Tougaloo College. By the spring of my second year, I was still picking up as many of my major classes as I could. The third year they let me move into the senior's dormitory. This was the only other dormitory for the young women during that time.

I took as many classes as I could during this time also. I picked up quite a few of my major classes, and by the third summer I had finished all of my required credits. I was now in the student teaching program.

The third summer was a fast study in moving toward the working world. These weeks were the last of the umbilical connection to the Eagle Queen, Tougaloo Christian College. The first six weeks of classes were with Dr. J.R. Shannon for Supervised Teacher Training. The last six weeks were spent in Hollandale, Mississippi for the onsite, Student Teaching units. This was how I spent my last summer session.

It was at this time that my participation, along with the others who participated as the Tougaloo Nine and other students in general, had to face some of the fall-out from our actions. This revelation was later discovered when some students from Tougaloo found it difficult to find places for student teaching other than the Delta Area where *Jim Crow* and *cotton was King*. I taught during the summer in the hot sweltering Delta heat but I will share this part of my experience with you later. Of all the colleges, I have attended since; Tougaloo was the best experience by far. I had the opportunity to be a teacher of Physical Education and Dance while I was still a student. The hands on participation as a major leading exercises and refereeing games helped me build my confidence in teaching physical education in the employment and volunteer teaching that I had an opportunity be a part of. Who wouldn't like to have had an opportunity like that?

As a Physical Education Major, my freshman classes in activity allowed me to assist other Majors lead exercises. This was always a favorite part of being a Physical Education Major. We got the opportunity to have leadership very early in our educational studies.

I formed a Dance Troupe and soon performed with the group at every opportune moment. We presented the *Nutcracker Suite* for the first two years during the Christmas season, which was our own production. My parents and neighbors from Ray Street attended several of my Dance Productions on Tougaloo Campus. I was so proud and they were proud of me.

The best part of the Dance Troupe was the autonomy in planning the dances as well as selecting the music, practicing in the spacious gymnasium, and performing our stylized choreography to the delight of our audiences. We also performed during basketball half times, on some occasions during basketball season. We were versatile and performed Impressionistic Dance, Modern Dance, and Ballet. We used music from some of the best artist we could find, including Jazz, Blues and Pop genres. Our Troupe was small but dedicated. One of our dancers was a young man who was studying to be a minister. Wow, could he dance. I share this fact with you because of his chosen field of study. How he finally made his calling as a minister is something I cannot share with you, because we lost contact. During our Dance Troupe experiences his name was all the rage, for his popular personality. He was also one of the fraternity members of the mighty Kappa's on campus. Yes, there were the Omegas and the Alphas but most of my male friends and associates were Kappa. When my partner danced we talked and kept a straight face. What we said was something like this, I would say, "man you almost dropped me on that catch" and he would make a statement in return to the outcome, "but you landed on your feet!" We would smile with our teeth showing and hoped that no one in the audience knew the steps we missed or miss-stepped.

The Dance Troupe and other responsibilities allowed me a great time and great experiences those days on Tougaloo College Campus. Upon finishing my B.S. degree, I was offered a scholarship to the University of Michigan in Dance. Although I did not attend the University of Michigan, I did follow-up later in life. I did develop my dance techniques as I taught many units of dance in the courses of Physical Education, over my teaching career. I also incorporated my desire for stunts and tumbling into what I later learned was *Gymnastics*. I had no formal training from college but during my teaching career I participated through workshops and college credit courses, full spectrum of Gymnastics as a performer, teacher, coach and Judge for junior high school boys and girls and high school girls. Gymnastics is an individual sports activity that can also be a team contribution.

My personal choices of sports while in college were individual sports: Archery and Tennis. I had to also participate in team activities which consisted of basketball, softball, volleyball and badminton. Table Tennis was a great recreational game that I enjoyed even to this day. The coach taught many of the major classes and I found myself one of the few girls in classes with the male football and basketball athletes. Classes were held in the team planning room in the back of the gymnasium. There were a lot of strategies and game plans discussed and thrown around. Because of the fact that I was not as knowledgeable on their level on plays and game strategies my grades did suffered. I did not get the A's I desired to get in those athlete-dominated classes. There was a female Professor who also taught major courses. Both professors taught Kinesiology. Many of my major classes were also in the Science Department. This was all doable as I stuck with the program in order to make my goal of three years and three summers. By the grace of God, I was successful.

I share with you now that the plan was a successful one. However, there were some very extenuating circumstances to contend with for the entire three years and three summers. I shared that I seem to thrive on challenges. However, the beginning of my second year of studies at Tougaloo was difficult because my mom had breast cancer and went through all of the operations, chemo and other treatments while I was away at college. She tried to keep as much of her treatments as she could from me but somehow I learned about them. I knew from other family members what was happening as her treatment progressed. During the winter break I needed to heal from a serious physical condition and needed a lot of rest. While I was home for the vacation time, Mom and I shared her bedroom recuperating together. We talked and bonded deeply during these weeks. I am grateful for the time we spent together. Little did I even imagine that her life span would be so very short! Before I go on with my story I want to reveal to you the fact that she passed at the age of forty one. This fact instilled in me the quest to live everyday to the fullest. To give of myself, my time, influence and means to uplift and mentor when and where ever I could. This experience of my mother's bout with cancer happened in my second year and before I was a part of the Tougaloo Nine Event. I really shared the experience to make you aware of the challenges I faced during this second year.

Being the oldest and first girl had its benefits and challenge. I had no regrets for my decisions or my actions. *I do continue to be appreciative for my life experiences and even the results.* It was not just me. It was family, the life experiences and the blessings from God almighty. My mother always gave me the opportunity to grow in many areas such as self-confidence, which was evident in my attendance to Tougaloo College. She encouraged me in self-realization to accept what I did accomplish as in the quest to make my goal to finish college in three years and three summers. She guided me into self—appreciation to feel positive about who and what I was able to accomplish in spite of the challenges I encountered while in college.

As I looked over my life, I see clearly how my mom's interventions helped me in my developments for successful living skills. This was especially true as I grew and developed during my years at Tougaloo College. I was not always receptive but it was and continues to be acknowledged that she was a great inspiration in who I eventually became. I will always be eternally grateful for the love, guidance, nurturing and Christian teachings of my mother. The method and reason my mom gave me responsibilities and trust in my early days, even when we lived in Orange, Texas has helped me. What she did and I later realized was essentially to give me the life skills that have helped me in my overall development. The participation in the Tougaloo Nine Non-Violent Historical Civil Disobedience Event changed all of our lives for the better. Yet, in spite of what I learned from my experiences, it was my feeling that the immediate results from the police were with unwarranted consequences. The action landed us in jail which we were anticipating and with *a mug shot* that can be accessed for eternity which I did not anticipate, now that we are in the digital information age. The experience and resulting actions did not deter me because my long-term goals were set in my mind in the beginning of my quest for a higher education. My goal for the future was to help my family and to put myself in a position to provide funds for my next brother as well as myself. My desire was always to be self-sustaining even before I knew the meaning of the term. So much has been shared about my experiences prior to and while in college, yet the heavy part of self-sustaining has only touched the surface.

PART 4: CHALLENGING THE STATE OF MISSISSIPPI FOR EQUITY ON BEHALF OF ALL CITIZENS.

Chapter 9

The Invitation, The Forums, The Selection and Eventual Acknowledgment!

The Invitation

If God be my helper, I want you to know how I got to that place and time on March 27, 1961 during my second year in college. I want to share with you how I dealt with the fall out and consequences of my actions in this historical life changing event. Along with other students during that time, college gave me the same opportunity to have a desire and goal to succeed. To be able to have a career and leave the mentality of the Jim Crow Era, I had to increase my educational level. In order to meet this challenge, I found that there were distractions.

There was the new experience of being away from home, missing family and the usual circumstances and things that I was used to. It made a difference when I left the nurturing family, extended family and the kitchen pantry. Nothing is more of a shock than when you get hungry for munches in the middle of the night, or after finishing a dining room bag snack. The bag lunch that was to carry you over from the Sunday mid-day meal until the next Monday morning breakfast call and realize it is only 10:00 p.m. on Sunday night. It only took a few weeks that first year before I was calling home for reinforcements and some of Mom's baked cookies. Mom did not disappoint with a letter each week or a boxed package at least once a month until the Thanksgiving holiday.

Wow, it was so good to be able to go home and hang out with the family. Before I left, I teased all of my five brothers. What I told them was that, they would miss me, the snacks I made and nagging them to do this and do that. In the meantime, it was me who had missed them so very much that first two months at Tougaloo. But, it did not take long for me to get the hang of the college rhythm. Being freshmen also had its challenges. I will not dwell on this because it was different for each individual. I found the classrooms and the lecture halls a new method of instructional delivery. The research needed for assignments started very early. The Library became more than just a place to find books to read for pleasure and entertainment. Now, I used the Library to search and study more in-depth. It was a long way from my earlier library usage and the socializing study halls of high school. Although I did not make study hall a part of my school experience, the Library usage was more of satisfying my personal quest to know more about the world, the people and how things evolved. Now the library was a place to find out why and how it all worked.

Actually, I found all kinds of distractions very early in the freshman year. There were activities, shopping and the weekly trips to Jackson, Mississippi on the college school bus. I found handsome young men waiting on the sidewalks to and from the dormitory, waiting to see if they could get your attention and more. I found the canteen and café outside of the college gates. I found the many cigarette salesmen handing out sample packs of Camels and Salem's packed four to a box. There were other distractions, such as the Greek sisters who were inviting you to their socials in dormitories. Then there was the coveted schedule designed especially for me. I knew that this schedule was not like the others in the school and I felt closeness and endearment because it had been designed just for me. It was my desire to follow this schedule exactly if possible in order to finish my coursework in the three years and three summers.

I finished the first year with good grades and credits. I finished the first two summer sessions, taking the classes outlined on the schedule. It was a challenge to make certain that I took those classes that were offered and would take care of all my basic and core requirements.

I studied and yes, I played. Remember, I was a Physical Education Major. When I use the term play, I mean it literally as well as figuratively. In other words, I was an active individual. My second year was somewhat more of a real challenge. I was taking upper class credits. My mom was ill. As you can see I had enough going on in my life to be highly distracted. Yet, I was working very hard, keeping up the public profile that all was well. Okay, it was not always well. I slowed down on activities, especially, if they were not academic. But I needed to be connected to something to challenge my mental and emotional status. Male companionship was not the answer, because I was not making that kind of choice as a serious consideration. So, what else was there and at a price I could afford?

A solution to this need came in 1961, when I got an invitation during my second year at Tougaloo to join the group of youth that were a part of the Youth NAACP. I became a member and got my membership pin which is still in my procession. At that time I was already an active participant in the weekly forums held in the Sociology Lab next door to the dormitory.

The Forums

It was after the winter break in my second year that I seriously started attending the Sociology Forums in the hall next door with Dr. Burinski. Dr. Burinski was the head of the Sociology Department; my belief was that, he was of German decent, as were several other Professors. German was my chosen foreign language. I had to take the class for two years. From time to time, Dr. Burinski would speak in German. At the least, I was able to get the feel for his pronunciations' because of his accent. The weekly forums were enlightening and a change of pace for me. As you can see, from all of my experiences, there was maximization of all of my intents. The forums were a peek into the thoughts of many speakers from across the nation. There were even some from abroad. Sometimes I would come close to the end but made it a point to attend as much as I could. It was also a social hour afterwards with day old donuts, coffee or tea. It was definitely a turning point for me. I was in contact with the student NAACP, Joseph Jackson who was also a Philosophy Major. Joseph impressed me in the beginning as a serious student. I was drawn to serious students, as I was to my friend from SVT. Dr. Mangram, our chaplain was one of our leaders. Megar Evers was an advisor in the Mississippi NAACP. Yes, it was a different time.

When the students were selected to participate in the demonstration, I was one of those chosen. There were criteria for being chosen. At the time I was identified as the daughter of a Pastor. He was the leader of small church with a small congregation. He was also an employee of the Natchez International Paper Mill. He was a small family business owner. The business was a family operated gas station, sundry and recreational area where teens, young adults and community members hung out. The beverages were non-alcoholic and there was a small menu of burgers, hotdogs and cold sandwiches. There were pool tables, pinball machines and of course a jukebox. All of these games generated the coveted quarters that amounted to a small sum of dollars to keep the recreational area open. My mom, dad, and brother John, operated, *the place* as we still call it. Since it was family, the younger ones were there for a great part of the time. It seemed like we were a *self-supporting* family. We really were much more liable than I knew at the time. The Forums got me started but to stay and be selected had a lot to do with who I was and my family life.

The Selection

Before we made the decision to participate in the Jackson Library sit-in, I called my family to let them know that I was going to be a part of *something* and not to worry. I assured them that I was okay in school and that the call was just to let them know that I would be okay. This part of my story includes the forums because this was the key to having a place to meet, congregate, and become inspired by the speakers who had something to share on those Wednesday nights. The forums and were held after classes and the supper time. I really cannot tell you all of the individual speakers but I got the concept that something needed to be done in the state of Mississippi to stop the injustice that was rampant in the state of Mississippi.

That invitation was the beginning of something spectacular. The specifics are documented in history. The popular magazines of the time were Time, Newsweek, Ebony, and Jet, The Today, Look and many others periodicals. They all documented the Tougaloo Nine's actions of March 27, 1961. Yet my feelings are locked away in memory. They are still there and waiting to *escape*. This phase of my life was so emotional and it has been very hard for me to talk about it until now.

I alluded to it over the years but depending on the audience response, it was perceived by me as an underappreciated subject. It was as if it had no real meaning to the associates and co-workers I found myself around for so many years. I do believe that my feelings were that it was no point to even talk about the experience once I was in California. Before, I came to California in the late '60s, fellow Mississippians were reluctant to talk about the event or even afraid to openly discuss the issues. The attitudes of both blacks and whites were not yet used to the idea of equal status for all individuals.

Yet, this information was inside of me. It was a part of who I was and a part that was not validated for what I attempted to do. I was proud of what I did, yet I was hurt and angry about the event. There was simply no acknowledgement of our involvement in opening up the state of Mississippi. Over the years of returning to Mississippi, I had not one conversation about the actions of the Tougaloo Nine's contribution to the slow turning towards acceptance in fellow Mississippians due to constitutional mandate. My feeling were compressed, bruised and withheld. Now I want to let my feeling out. I want to talk about the experience. To tell everyone who will listen, hear me and perhaps relate to what I experienced. Yes, dang it, as my granddad, Alfred, would say, because he never used profanity. I was selected to be a part of this historical event and now you know that much. There is more that I want you to know after the fact of the selection. I have much more to tell you about the next important steps. But I also want to yell and scream to you that I made a difference in the lives that you now enjoy and you do not even know that I lived well in spite of the challenge that propelled me on this journey of dynamic, *change*!

Eventual Acknowledgment!

At one Sadie V. Thompson Era Reunion early in 2000, an old flame approached me and although his wife was close by to me, asked me, "Do you remembered who I am"? Yes, it was the manner in which he asked the question. I looked at him in his eyes, of his now puffed face that was once chiseled and clean. My respond was, "yes, and?" And with a turned head without hesitation, I gave my attention back to my friend girl with whom I came. I gave him no satisfaction with a follow-up, of conversation or body language because he did not acknowledge me as a contributor for the life style he was privy to enjoy at this time. My feelings were, if he remembered me, it would have been great to at least acknowledge my sacrifice to his lifestyle that he was able to enjoy from that time up to that present moment. He was also rebuked for the fact that I was someone to be remembered for more than my femininity!

In 2006, I was finally able to physically, mentally and financially because I was retired and freer to meet the challenge of public acknowledgement. The invitation came to assemble at Tougaloo College's Founders Week Celebration. The Tougaloo Nine were invited as special guests for several appearances during the week. This was on the 45th Anniversary of the event *that propelled the group into history and changed lives for all who lived in the state of Mississippi.* The event changed the nation because Mississippi was always believed to be . . . the last to change from the *status quo.* If you know anything about the history of Mississippi, you can remember the extent the Governor at the time showed his disdain for Blacks and Whites who attempted to make a change in Mississippi. The Freedom Riders, who rode into Mississippi in May, after the Tougaloo Nine successful event were imprisoned and tormented emotionally and physically. This act made in March of 1961 was successful because it was first to start the change in injustice and it was definitely not expected. As a member of the Tougaloo Nine, we made this statement with our participation, that we were a group to be recognized and acknowledged! This successful challenge prompted the powers of the governing body and the media in general to make the following acknowledgment. "The proponents of Segregation, Separate but Equal keep the *Coloreds* in their place and all the other beliefs and expectations from the powers that were, did not expect the bombshell that the Tougaloo *Nine* Students dropped, On March 27, 1961." (Jackson Mississippi Boycotts, web links n.d.)

Chapter 10

The Mentality, The Planning and The Preparation!

The Mentality

I was apprehensive but had no fear for my life, my status at Tougaloo or even my future, at that time. One of the points that came out about criteria in asking for our participation was the ability to take the risk, stay calm and be obedient. To succeed this was paramount! There was to be no resistance. Could I do this? Yes! With my life experiences so far, I was divinely prepared to be a part of this *Jackson White-only Library Historical Event.* At this particular time in history, there was a significant desire to find acceptance of blacks, *Negros* to be treated justly, along with the ability to live and contribute to the wellbeing of our state of Mississippi. When you were a scholar of life and knew the circumstances under which we lived as a *Colored*, you were already informed. When you knew more about the injustice and deprivation in this stately, historical community, as compared to the desired life through enlightenment, it is difficult to remain silent. It was no longer acceptable to exist with the status quo. It was of the mindset that just because it was done this way, it continues to be right! We, the Tougaloo Nine had the opportunity, motive, youth and tenacity to challenge the mentality of the state of Mississippi to make a change.

The state of Mississippi is a beautiful state. The people are friendly and caring in general. There are great natural resources. However, my take on the matter was that with our intervention one day, Mississippi would be proud to be a part of the justice for all mentality. All that was needed was to eliminate the mindset of segregation, second-class citizenship and *separate but equal*, because it was an untruth. Given the opportunity, Mississippi could be bigger and better than the hate of blacks just because of the color of *our* skins. Underneath, the ever present Sovereignty cloud of ignorance men, women, boys and girls are all children of God! It was all a state of mind. Mississippians had a mentality that was destined to be changed. The Tougaloo Nine initiated the change!

The Planning

We met with our advisors; Medgar Wiley Evers, whose lifespan was from 1925-1963. John Mangram was Chaplain of Tougaloo College from 1950 to 1961. They were the connection with the official groups that would sponsor the logistics of the planned participation. This event had the history of what had happened in similar attempts to change the status quo in other regions of the Southern States. It was a known fact that the citizens and governing body of Mississippi felt that they were too entwined in the segregated lifestyle to be challenged by *Coloreds*. Mississippians voiced their superior stance on the color code with assurance. We needed some strong advisors and leaders to pull the planned capper off. Thankfully we had both Medger Evers and John Mangram who were dedicated to the cause at hand. With their guidance our task was to make our plans for a safe and successful event. We knew that we were embarking on a life changing experience. Many of us were chosen because of our parents' position or status in our home community. My father was a minister, but he also worked at the International Paper Mill. From what I remember, many others in the group were also from families of ministers and owners of various businesses. John Mangram, our chaplain and advisor in support of our preparation, made certain that we were adequately prepared for the event. We had a serious task and although we were young, we knew the breadth and depth of this historical event. We had to know why we were making this stance for social justice. We had to count the cost of what may have been our personal fate. John Mangram led us in faith and dedication with prayers for our successful intervention. We had to stand for our own rights to live and have our being as any other citizen of this state and country at large. We were young but we were informed because we lived in this unjust society that was ripe for a change. Chaplain Mangram supported our decisions as he guided us to work the non-violence philosophy. Both advisors directed us to respect the desire for people to want to live free. We too wanted acceptance of the constitutional inevitable right to live and be and have our being as any other citizen in these United States of America. This was our goal in the planning and implementation of this event.

The preparation

We were directed to prepare our minds, heart and body as we opened the door of communication with our families to give them the opportunity to anticipate a change that we would be a part of. We were instructed to call our parents and tell them not to be surprised at anything they may hear but we were not to tell them exactly what we were going to do. To my knowledge no parental consent was given. We were all over the age of eighteen and were enrolled in College. We were drilled in the non-violent philosophy, proposed and mentored by Dr. Martin Luther King, Jr. As students at Tougaloo College, we were privileged to have an outstanding Social Science Department consisting of the most outstanding minds of the decade. They presented the forums used to incite our thinking. We had great minds and support. We had the historical belief of Dr. Martin Luther King, Jr. Following the safe and clear outline of non-violence was our first goal. National media coverage of our every step in this process was our next move. To breach the stronghold of segregation was to be delivered with dignity, pride and above all to be non-violent.

Some of the students in the preparation along with our advisors were not all participants in the event. They were Mary Allen, Meredith Andings Jr., James "Sammy" Bradford, Joan Collins, Alfred Cook, Janice Jackson, Joseph Jackson, who was the president of the college NAACP, Albert Lassiter, Evelyn Pierce, Ethel Sawyer, and yours truly, Geraldine Edwards. There may have been others but it is difficult to remember all of the names after these fifty years and for that, my apologies!

That this happened at Tougaloo Southern Christian College, *the correct name when I first enrolled,* is no accident. Tougaloo College, *as it is now known* is and continues to be a developer and promoter of leadership in all areas of education, endeavors and participation. Our mentality, planning and preparation were in line with the philosophy of developing leadership. Our deportment and representation was for the good of our students, community, town, state and the nation. Did we know that our event would resound world-wide?

Chapter 11

The Event and The Action

What do you wear to an event that you do not know the results? Clothing and how you look is very important. It was the policy of the college that all young ladies leave campus dressed in heels, stockings, and even gloves. My choice was an appropriate dress and jacket or a suit. This was considered the appropriate attire for all ladies when going into town, *Jackson, MS*.

The Event

For the occasion, I chose to wear a suit that I designed and sewed. I wore a two piece double breasted outfit which had a comfortable feel. It was warm and had three-quarter length sleeves. For the cool weather, I needed more coverage. I chose my green raincoat with matching cap. It was lined, water-proofed and made of poplin cotton. There were pockets to put things in for safekeeping. As a result, I was dressed for the weather and any circumstances that may have occurred.

Aware that there may be bodily harm, the one good thing about reading was that you could find out what was happening in other parts of the South. It was known by all nine of us what had transpired in Arkansas and Tennessee with other students.

They were chosen to integrate schools in those Southern States. It was a known fact that force was used in situations where sit-ins were held. I knew the police used dogs, *to control peaceful civil disobedience*! Being prepared with the knowledge that the major news media had been contacted, the event was planned with precision. In reality, this was major in every aspect.

On March 27, 1961, I followed the instructions we were given. Preparing for this experience was not something to be left to too much chance. I knew exactly what my assignment was and was ready to carry it out. I knew that I had a certain book title that would not be in the *Colored Library* when we first went there. Medger Evers and Chaplain John Mangram were there in the background to get us where we needed to go. I may not remember exactly how we got to the two libraries. I do remember being confronted by the detectives. They asked me to leave. This was when I knew that I had no *fear*. All of my life I was confronted with opposition to be free to do what I saw others (Whites) doing. I was afraid for my situation but the fear was gone. My emotions were replaced with the determination to do this. I would read in this library or suffer the consequences for my innate choice to do so.

Growing up in Orange, Vidalia and Natchez, I always had a mind to do all that I was capable of doing. This time was no different! I made my choice to participate and by doing so made the choice to live with the consequences.

The Action

We were able to breech the Jackson Public Library on March 27, 1961. We accomplished our goal of getting a book and sitting down in this *white only public library*. They took me away. They led me out of the building. I knew that there were three other young ladies and five fellows. It seemed to be one or more detective for each of us. I walked out with them but the *fear* was gone. They took me away but could not take away my dignity. My head was held high. I did not have any reason to be ashamed. As I went along with the group, I glanced around to take in the interior of the building. It far exceeded those I had visited on other occasions. Our sit-in was necessary for the preservation of educational growth of all who desired it. It was my belief that I had the right to all that others enjoyed on a daily basis. It was my belief that I too had the right that all individuals are created equal and that the color of our skin should not represent our mind. When we exited from the library we had a revelation of what we were to be faced with. We were faced with guns, dogs, and angry verbalizations. We were put into police cars and driven to the city jail. We were booked into jail after some bad mug shots. Thankfully, we had good media coverage. We had the tour of the Jackson city jail and were given residence for some days. This is what happened and it was difficult to talk about it then and even to this day. I did share my story in spurts over time and to small audiences. You be the judge. How and what more can I say, other than, "The Tougaloo Nine made a difference"!

My statements more than once, shared with you that there was a problem for me to talk about the actions that I experienced. Even now, it is so very emotional for me.

It is for this reason, that I included this dialog in my manuscript. I like the description given by Kwame, the son of the Northern

California Alumni Association President, Janice Wilson in his blog-spot in 2010. He heard what I said. He felt what my story meant to him as well as the others I was speaking to. He may not have known that he would be so moved to make this blog. He came to do just one thing for the Northern California Tougaloo College Alumni Chapter (NCTCAC). He was invited to take photos of a Tougaloo College Alumni fundraising event but was moved to share with others what he learned as he listened to my talk about my experience in the Tougaloo Nine Event.

Kwame paraphrased what I shared with the supporters and Alumni at the fundraiser, held at the Delany Street Restaurant in San Francisco, CA. I think I use his words because I have always found it difficult to talk about myself. It was difficult when I found many not connecting with me on times that I did. I made attempts at church meetings and even while making a talk on Black History during the past ten years.

Kwame explained, *"She (Geraldine Edwards Hollis) told the story of a small group of Tougaloo College students that decided it was time for a change. And on March 27th, 1961 they did something about it. Nine students from Tougaloo College went to the Carver Library to request some books. Knowing the books would not be available, they peacefully went to the Jackson Public Library, to find the books they requested. They retrieved the books and began reading them. In 1961, this was a very bold move for nine black students to leave the "Black only" Carver Library and step foot inside the "White only" Jackson Public Library. This was in fact illegal and the nine students were arrested and held for over 30 hours in jail. This act, this peaceful act of sitting in the library (a sit-in), help start the major change that was needed in Mississippi and all over the South. Her name is Geraldine Hollis, formerly, Geraldine Edwards, and she is one of the Tougaloo Nine.!"*

(Kwame 2010)

This strong emotional feeling that overcome me each and every time that I have to share what, how, when and why, I am relieved to have someone who can relate to this and tell others about it. This is especially true if I shared with this individual from my prospective and they felt the emotions that I evoked in them and were moved to tell others.

As the Northern California Tougaloo College Alumni Chapter, made its debut fundraiser, I had made my public debut revelation of this historical leadership participation. I was delighted to see that Kwame published this dialog in his blog for the 21th Century to read. Kwame picked up on my emotions and was moved as I shared the story to the group of supporters of The Tougaloo Alumni. This was great validation for me especially since this was the first time someone was so moved to repeat what I shared. I feel appreciative because the action was documented in history for all to read and see.

Chapter 12

Incarceration!

My decisions that I made in my life were mine to make because for as long as I can remember my desire was always to be a self directed and spirited person. I knew that what we did was against the law of the land but was it right to continue to deny anyone access to public facilities? It was a denial of my rights to see other kids, *whites* walking or just going to schools in their neighborhoods and I had to walk past those schools. I could not attend those certain schools and had to go to another on the other side of town. This was not a choice but a lifestyle because of the color of my skin. In Vidalia, we lived on the north side of town and had to walk all the way to the south side to school.

As a girl I wanted to go to the Vidalia Pharmacy soda fountain and get an ice cream soda. I wanted to sit in the fancy metal chairs while being allowed to sip my treat. This was not to happen. The little white girls and their families enjoyed this treat. They were just like me, except for the fact that I was *colored*. In Natchez during the time that I went to Broomfield school, I had to walk from the north past two white schools to the south-east to get to school. There were no buses for the school district and during that time not even transit buses. We had to walk everywhere when we did not get a ride in someone's car. We walked in hot and cold weather.

Rain, sleet and storms did not make a change for me and my family. We had to walk but we did benefit physically. Endurance is what we gained and was something that was learned. So let's get back to the incarceration process.

The booking into jail was a bad snap shot of me, both front and side. This is why it is called a *Mug* shot. You do not get a chance to prepare with a smile or even focus. They finger printed me and escorted me to a cell. Although the members of the Tougaloo Nine went into the library together, the booking was an individual part of the process. I remember being in a cell bare and smelly with soiled flat mats. I had endured the outhouse at home and at school while living in Vidalia, but this rivaled that smell by far. The stench penetrated my nostrils like a sharp object. There is something sickening about accumulated and foul body odors. The cell was divided in two sections. Two of us young ladies were in one and the other two in the other across from us. I do not know what they did with the young men.

To pass the time away, I danced and made fun of our situation. Dancing was something that I could do with or without music. I could dance in a large or small space. So to pass the time away for a large period of the time I was jailed, I danced. We had to be lighthearted and strong because we knew that this would be our fate. We were locked up in a jail that held individuals that may have robbed or killed. What was our crime? Why were we here? I knew the answer to why I was incarcerated and I could live with that fact. For being a black citizen and not obeying the law of living as a second-class citizen under the Mississippi race rules of life, I was a violator. We did not know what was happening on the outside of the jail while we were locked up and we did not know for how long. Sleep came but rest was impossible. The conditions in the jail were worst than, "living dirt poor". I do not remember eating. I do not remember cleaning myself up. I do not know how long we were there. *I still say that it was 72 hours. Some report that it was only 30 hours . . . It felt more like 72 hours!* Time collapsed into a fog. My body and my mind became separated for a time. I needed to do this to remain safe and mentally sound.

During the time we were in jail, I think someone came to visit but I cannot be sure. It really was a fog. *I experienced an out of body experience.* It was hard to adjust with not being able to tell night from day. I was tired, exhausted and trying to keep a sense of sanity. It was a challenge to stay strong, to stay the course and yet not know what the future held. This was truly an uncertain time. The unknown is always scary but this was different. I experienced the unknown when I attended a new school in the various towns where I lived. But, I had the freedom to look around and the security to know that it was not to my harm. The jailing was an uncertainty and also posed a harm that I may not even live through. In all things and in every way, there were risks and the unknown. The raw fear of being in jail was something I would not recommend to anyone as a lifestyle. This I do know; that I was determined to stay upbeat in my mind. My body caved as it weathered the storm of incarceration but I survived.

My name was Geraldine Edwards, in case you do not know that by now. I was a student in my second year at Tougaloo Christian College, Tougaloo Mississippi. You may know the prior statement by now but what you need to know about the group of us who were incarcerated for our civil rights, is a little specific information about the school that we attended. This Prestigious Historical Black College may not be as well known as Howard or Spellman, but for those of us who attended, it was and continues to be a Mecca for higher learning, excellence in living at the best you could be. The teachers were dedicated and at the time of my attendance in '59 to '62 had some of the most diverse faculty members I have ever seen in such a small school; most lived, and taught on the campus. The school was inclusive in that it was self-sustaining and self-supporting of all in the community which was also, Tougaloo. The basis for all students was Philosophy, and Chapel was a place as well as a way of life. It was not a surprise that I was a part of the planned civil disobedient activity. It was a surprise that I was incarcerated, because all of my life I never knew of any close family member to go to jail. We were law-abiding citizens. I did what was most unusual at that time, March 27, 1961. Unusual because there were nine students who felt the same inclination that I felt. My fellow schoolmates and I went to jail for breaching this forbidden hall of learning, the White-only Library in Jackson, Mississippi. We were called, The Tougaloo Nine and I was a part of this change agent for justice and freedom for all mankind, black and white, the *Tougaloo Nine.*

What I did at that time is a part of who I am. What I did at that time gave men, women, boys and girls the opportunity to live their lives with the right to vote without the Poll Tax. You may not be aware of this fact. Intimidating oral questions were asked out loud for all to hear, in order for black citizens to, *pass the exam to vote.* Since there was separation of the races, I can't be certain that there were no, oral tests for the whites. But, from my readings, other states did not require the same procedure for citizens to be able to vote. There were no known standardized oral tests for Negros, as blacks were called. The experience that I personally had with the oral tests was impromptu. It was definitely a race intimidation ploy. It was also common practice for anyone with African American blood, to be treated with such blatant disdain. The political structure was to humiliate the blacks and keep the constitutional right of voting only for the whites. What I did gave others the lack of fear and the opportunity to join in and support what we started. What I did affected college students, white and black so much so that they were willing to take buses to the south to continue to make a change using non-violent civil disobedience. What I did along with the other Tougaloo Nine students started the movement of integration in the Sovereign (Smile, because that is what they thought of themselves) State of Mississippi. What I was a part of took on a life of its own for a dramatic change.

The Reaction

The reaction of our sit-in in the Jackson Library, sparked Headlines in every major news media in the *whole world*, my description because, it was my world that was rocked. It was a wake-up call for Mississippians. It was a jolt also to The Southern Patriot, Published by the Southern Conference Educational Fund, Inc. because they wrote, "Jackson reaches Turning Point, As Negro Students Act." (Correspondent 1961) This headline was in its' Mississippi Report. This paper was a part of my collection from 1961 until I turned it over to Tougaloo College President, Beverly Hogan on the celebration of the 45th Anniversary. This statement that, *Jackson reaches a turning point* (Correspondent 1961) is the essence of why I needed to remind myself and you that the Tougaloo Nine made a tremendous difference in the State of Mississippi. All change offers emotional feelings such as hope or fear. It was a well known fact that the staff of this periodical knew that the black citizens of Mississippi were overwhelmingly filled with hope for the future. Yet, at the very same instance the white citizens were filled with fear due to the change of attitudes facilitated by the event. There was a reason to fear the loss of an erroneous feeling of superiority, at the expense of the black citizens. We are all God's children; black, white, yellow or red, every one of us deserved respect and the equality, alive or even dead!

We were simple college students who braved the fear factor and crossed the line of racial divide. We were called courageous young students but, my schoolmates and I simply stepped out to take our stand for full civil rights. No more degradation, separate but equal, second class citizenship, denial of the right to vote and equal protection from the hooded cowards known as the Klu Klux Klan (KKK) would be tolerated as normal. This action of non-violence civil disobedience was what was required. This was how we felt about the task handed to us and this was what we did. I was there and I wanted all that change to happen. There was something really courageous about being the first to do something, especially if it involved a large degree of risk.

The response and reactions of the white citizens at the time was mixed and with good cause. This situation was more than new to many of them. It was the beginning of the end results that they had not envisioned since the beginning of the reconstruction period right after blacks were freed from slavery. Surely, it was a time that white Mississippians had to come to the realization that, their own freedom depended on recognition and respect for the deep desire of the *Black Citizens* for dignity. One thing was certain: regardless of their wishful thinking to remain as they always were, the whites had to realize the blacks' discontent. As was evident in the successful stand made by the Tougaloo Nine, the student movement did not go away! One of our fellow Tougaloo Nine participants, when asked why we did what we did on March 27, 1961 had this to say, "We do not hate those who oppose us; we blame it on ignorance. We grew up in Mississippi and we know these people; (or we know their mentality) (Correspondent 1961) we are sorry for them."

We acknowledged our involvement by our actions. We started something that was normal for the rest of the United States: freedom and Civil Rights for all citizens, regardless to their creed or color. What the whites reacted to was their fear of losing something that was not theirs to have. Now the white citizens had to interact rather than react. So, there was only a little amount of credence for reaction. Do you agree that this was right?

The Support

Our presiding President of Tougaloo College, Dr. A. D. Beittel, took a stance for our actions. We were not expelled from college as our friends and supporters at Jackson State College, now University. Supporters called for a *Prayer Vigil* on our behalf. Expulsion was the action taken by their own college President, for their show of civil support. The students expelled were, sisters Dorie and Joyce

Landers and Student President, Walter Williams. This sparked the Jackson boycott and the continued Mississippi Movement.

Meanwhile, Tougaloo College Students *had* supported the effort with all that they were able and allowed to do. Food collected and sent to the Tougaloo Nine was undeliverable, as were flowers and any other method of physical support. We had the emotional support and love of which we were very appreciative. We found this out after we were released and upon returning to Tougaloo Campus. In a document, Dr. Beittel recorded that the Tougaloo Officials were against paying court fines which may be levied against The Tougaloo Nine. All were of the mindset that this would be worked out eventually. He wrote in his report, that a similar incident at a library in Memphis Tennessee had been opened to all its citizens. (Mississippi Digital Library n.d.) This was the basis of our justification and purpose which supported the Tougaloo Nine actions. (Mississippi Digital Library n.d.).

Chapter 13

Aftermath of Incarceration in Jackson and other parts of Mississippi!

The goals of the power that be, was to not have integration in the state of Mississippi. There were all kinds of tactics used to discourage and dissuade participants bent on making a change. The facts that the tools of provoking fear were German shepherd dogs, water sprayed from fire hydrants and cruel beatings were all a possibility for The Tougaloo Nine. It was discussed and we all knew the risk that we embarked on. That same determination that propelled me to skate out of my all black residential area, to ride all over the small town of Vidalia was the same determination that was evident when I agreed to follow the plan to be involved in the movement. My resolve was that there had always been an unjust and unequal difference in the blacks and whites. The inner self always asked the question, why? But the ideology was not to rock the boat. As a child I knew that I did not like to say, "Yes madam" to a white girl my same age but that was the expected and courteous response to the whites. To be honest, I never had a real conversation with a white boy or girl until we moved to Mississippi. The white family was the ones who operated the local gas station on Pine Street and also lived in the back area of the business.

This family had no other home and they did not own the business. We also found out that the dad was a high ranking KKK member. They attended school and did not walk because the station was surrounded by blacks. Their parents drove them to school and they had only to go about a mile. We on the other hand had to walk miles to school past the schools for the whites. The children talked to us in the play area because they had no other children around to talk to. Their playground was the same bayou that we played in, which ran right behind the gas station and their back yard was the bayou. We met in the bottom and played together. When we went into the store part of the gas station we had an understanding. In front of their parents and patrons, they had nothing to say to us. It was an interesting way of life that we lived. The dad's activities in the Klan were made known somehow to the black community. After being identified as a Klansman there was a change in the attitude of everyone towards the business.

The dad had to soften his stance of how he treated the blacks when he found his livelihood threatened. The blacks took their business elsewhere and started a small boycott of the gas station. Sometimes the economical state can make the living more equitable when the livelihood is threatened. As blacks in Mississippi, we learned this.

The changes that have occurred over time in Mississippi are more visible because of The Tougaloo Nine. The celebration of the event was because of the success for all citizens. Our group of five men and four women touched off the major civil rights movement in the city of Jackson.

My statement regarding the aftermath was made and was recorded at the Celebration Forum in Woodworth Chapel, after forty five years. My quote, as reported by Cheryl Lasseter of WLBT channel 3, was "In my family, I had a history of doing things first. I was the first to go to college, the first to do everything; I was the first to go to jail." (Cheryl Lassiter 2006) I ended the statement with a big laugh. Yes, after all those years, I could still laugh about the circumstances. I am thankful to God almighty for the opportunity to make a difference in the lives of so many!

The aftermath of the Jackson Library Sit-in was also acknowledged as a watershed event in the civil rights movement in Mississippi. It was the place the nine of us from the Historically Black Tougaloo College made headlines when we quietly sat in at the library located on State Street in the heart of downtown Jackson. The main branch served only *White Citizens*. At this very same time *Black Citizens* were sent to the substandard Carver Library. This simple act of civil disobedience began the organized protests against the Jim Crow system in Jackson. All of these facts were documented. (Web Links, Jackson Municipal Library/Hinds County n.d.) However, *my story* comes from me because it was capsulated in my memory. My task was to live my life as best I could. Now I am opening up to share my memories with you. These words are my goal of what I want to share with you. To do this successfully, I must move forward and do my best. My goal was for my siblings to have a better opportunity than I had. I envisioned a plan of support for my family as they had supported me in *Civil Disobedience*.

I was motivated to give back to society what I was not privileged to have at an earlier age. I knew that I was not given the opportunity that was afforded to other citizens, but I did not dwell on this. In fact, I was relieved that I was not beaten, hung or my family physically harmed. My dad, Rev. Simmel Edwards was physically and emotionally attacked. He was verbally denounced at his job, the International Paper Mill. The Klu Klux Klan, in their white pillowcases with holes cut for eyes, rode horses inside of our small family business which was a filling station with a teen center. The patrons and our family were inside when this happened. The KKK sent a message that, "we were to be afraid for our actions." Thank God that no bodily harm was done. Can you imagine today someone riding horses in your local Seven Eleven store? Or even a small fast food establishment? This is the scene that happened in our small family business. The mental and physical damage that was done was unwarranted. When individuals have an unwritten warranty to use their own decision to intimidate or even to maim black citizens under the cloak of a pointed hat or the veil of night, what more can be expected? This incident of brutal intrusion to intimidate was retold by neighbors who lived in and around the small family business for years after the incident. However, the message was not of fear. The message was that the KKK's desire to suppress the black citizens was weakened when we stepped into *their library*. The Tougaloo Nine took that first step of Non-violent Civil Disobedience in Mississippi. The Tougaloo Students, of which I was one of the Nine, made history in the state of Mississippi, these United States and resounded around the world.

Mississippi could not go back to segregation without the world taking notice. The governor at that time tried to maintain segregation. While they were still on the bus, he arrested the Freedom Riders. Their purpose was to facilitate integration in the state of Mississippi. No matter the tactics that were later taken, Jackson had experienced integration in the white only library on March 27, 1961, by my schoolmates and me.

My wish is that all citizens acknowledge that living together is better than existing together. Spend less, save more, borrow less and give more. To thy own self be true and uplift your neighbor no matter the color, creed or ethnicity!

Chapter 14

The Media, the Effect and the Results Produced by the Library Sit-in

The effect of the Jackson Library Sit-in was national news. The media really picked up on the event and made it known to the world by world-wide news. According to my family it was in several different news spots on the day that it occurred. My family found out because of the keen eyes and ears of my youngest brother, my birthday present brother, David Lawrence who was only 6 years old. He was watching television and by being alert shared with my mom that he saw me on television. They did not believe him at first but as the news repeated and the sensation of *Nine Black students, from Tougaloo College* really got their attention. They knew me and they remembered my phone call just a week or so prior to this *Event*.

Mom and Dad were even tempered individuals. Both were dedicated Christians. They were proud yet humble. They were compassionate as demonstrated when they took my friend to Tougaloo and acted as her advocate. They were alarmed at the news but not shocked. They demonstrated by doing in the community what I found as my chosen life path. My mom volunteered in the church as a youth advisor for the choir and also for the Bible study and as a Sunday school teacher. She was the First Lady to my dad who was the pastor of the church. Our entire family was members and they were prepared for much that happened to teenagers but this was a jolt! My parents were aware of my tenacity and probably did not expect this caliber of national news for what I was then involved in. Our entire family was involved because of who they were to me. At that time my brothers ranged from the eleventh grade down to the first grade. This meant that there was one of my brothers at every school level in Natchez segregated schools!

Our family business bore the effect because it was the scene of the hooded KKK riding horses inside the place. This act put the community at risk as teens, youth and other individuals were inside. They did not do any bodily harm but intended to make a statement about my participation in the Tougaloo Nine Library Sit-In. My dad stood his ground and was prepared with protection in the place as a business person dealing with cash receipts. He said that he was in the, *grace and mercy of God.*

Our neighbors on Ray Street were the same as always, supportive and encouraging. All of the family, friends and church members were supportive of my family's plight of having a daughter in the national news and making a dangerous choice to make a change in the *status quo* for civil rights for all who lived in our unjust society. The documentation of this event has been published in Ebony, Jet, and Time and on and on. The internet has picked up on the specifics as it evolved through search engines. True to realism, I cannot tell you something that I do not know. With documentation, I can share with you what the world saw at that event. You can be the judge of what the Tougaloo Nine endured.

I know that there was more than I could see while incarcerated but read my remembrances and imagine what the environment would be like for you.

Once we went into the white-only library, we did not talk to each other and followed our plan of an obedient, peaceful duty as assigned. My focus was on following what I was supposed to be doing. This was a challenge because we had all eyes on us. There were the all lily white staff and the white patrons who were in the library. There were the white officers and lastly, there was the media, who had been called and alerted regarding our planned participation. Had we not made those detailed plans, our peaceful participation would have been the same as some of the scenes in Selma and Montgomery, Alabama.

There were reports of threats of retaliation against Tougaloo Christian College and the President Dr. Beittel. He and his wife were loving and decent individuals, who could have been in danger. Not only for our sit-in but also because Tougaloo College was a safe haven for many who were in the civil rights movement. Tougaloo earned the name, *Cradle of Civil Rights!* Because that is what our college really was.

We did not know anything about the action of the Jackson State College students until after we were out of jail. I am grateful for the Jackson students who were compelled to be supportive. As we now know, the Jackson State students were not the only students mobilized by our actions in March 27th of 1961. We were proud to be the first pitch in the *World Series* for civil rights in the state of Mississippi. The Tougaloo Library Sit-in was a

Mississippi leadership moment that started the movement off to a roaring start. All students who participated in this era put their lives, schooling and families at risk. Someone had to do it. Someone had to start it. The very act was a course that changed the attitude of social injustice for blacks in Jackson, Mississippi and all of Mississippi. As individuals we languished in jail for our action and did not have any idea what our destiny would be as a result. We were thankful to God that we were unbeaten, unbitten and did not have broken bones or less teeth than when we went into the Library.

It was reported that on the following day, the Jackson State College students boycotted classes and held an illegal rally. This response was because they wanted to follow up on what we started. This continuing show of support fueled the Jackson Movement and solidified the fact that blacks were proud to let the white citizens and the world know that segregation was no longer tolerated in the state of Mississippi. The media coverage reported all of this for prosperity of enlightenment.

The reporting continued. The Jackson students marched towards the jail where we were being held. The Jackson State College students were then attacked by club-swinging police using tear gas and dogs to disperse them. Sadly, this was just the fate that we may have encounter had it not been for the element of surprise. Yes, they may have been alerted by the media influx, but the powers that were in charge felt that *Negros* as we were called would not rock the sound foundation of their laws. No blacks were allowed in any public facility via entrance of the front door except as a janitor or laborer. Not on their watch. Someone must have been asleep when we, the *Tougaloo Nine* made the bold entrance!

At the very same time that the Jackson State College students had the confrontation with the police there was another incident happening. This information is to let you see for yourself what was important to the white citizens of Mississippi at that time in history. Just a few blocks away it was reported that there were several thousand white marchers in Confederate uniforms, carrying rebel battle flags. Because of who they were, their right to celebrate was sanctioned by the then Governor, Ross Barnett. The governor was also reported to have proudly, been in attendance for the 100th anniversary of Mississippi's secession from the union in 1861. There was no confrontation as this event was being celebrated in large numbers by the white citizens. Please read this information carefully and compare the difference in what these events personified. The secession from the union celebration was of great importance to the majority of the southern white citizens. Celebration of their loss in the Civil War between the States was relegated to a high status and celebrated in a big way. There was pride to uphold and it was *pride* that made the successful intrusion into the library by the Tougaloo Nine so hard for the white citizens to swallow. So when the black students followed up in Jackson at the state college, the police had no other choice but to use the terrifying weapons that were theirs to use to show their superiority. The club swinging police also used tear gas and vicious dogs on innocent students and black citizens who dared show support for our event. What we did was a highly insulting show of non-violent civil disobedience by entering and sitting down to read a book in the white-only public library in the capital of Mississippi, Jackson.

It was reported in all the local newspapers that on our arrival at the courthouse we were cheered by a small crowd of black supporters. It was also reported that there were more supporters than had been able to squeeze into the *Colored* section of the courtroom. There was only a token amount of space allotted to the black citizens. Compared to other facilities in the separate but equal alignment of facilitation, the seating was probably the size of a postal stamp on a small regular envelope. The overflows of black supporters were attacked by the police officers, with clubs and dogs. This only enraged the black citizens more and caused them to turn out that night, as was later reported in a number that was more than 1,000, with them now being more black adults than students in support of the Tougaloo Nine. Myrtle Evers, the wife of Medgar Evers would later say of the Tougaloo Nine: *"The change of tide in Mississippi began with the Tougaloo Nine and the library sit-in."* (Web Links, New Programs to explore the Jackson-Area Civil Rights Movement n.d.)

It is naïve to say, that this is how the powers that be, felt about the infringement and inflaming of the library sit-in. The follow-up of the media and the infringement of their, *the white citizens*, protected, separate but equal facilities, along with their envisioned superior mindset infuriated the Jackson City Council. The police were again prompted to use the clubs and dogs when black citizens wanted to show their support for the Tougaloo Nine students. It was these very students who braved their raft in the beginning and started this *unwarranted integration* in the first place. It is my personal knowledge and belief, that Mississippi was braced for moving into the twenty-first century as separate but equal! You can be the judge, but history tells the story. We, *The Tougaloo Nine,* were not going on living as we were and that is why the event was planned and implemented with successful results. I can just imagine the white citizens saying, "How dare they stop what was already the acceptable and enjoyable way of life for us, the White Citizenry of the Sovereignty State of Mississippi!"

Part 5: After the Aftermath

Chapter 15

Life in the Aftermath of Civil Disobedience

For a week during the late spring of 1961, the Tougaloo Nine participants represented at the NAACP National Convention which was held in Philadelphia, Pennsylvania. This was one of the best things that came out of the Tougaloo Nine Sit-In. We all had the opportunity to share in word and deeds what we did in the Jackson, Mississippi Library Sit-in on March 27, earlier in the year. While at the NAACP National Convention in Philadelphia, PA we represented our chapter and attended the sessions. We met other youth chapter NAACP Members representing from all over the United States. This was a dynamic experience in the workings of the association and its' membership. I was also able to meet and talk with many of the Civil Rights movers and shakers. I shook hands with Dr. Martin Luther King, Jr. and was in his presence. I was also in the presence of Andrew Young and many others. I am not going to try to name all of the well known individuals that we were able to meet or to be in their presence. The mere fact that this convention happened in Philadelphia, PA and we were given the opportunity to attend was a treat as well as an honor.

I remember the hotel stay in the city of Philadelphia, and some of the other young students from all over the United States. While we were in attendance at the conference, we were also able to go by train to Washington, DC on the Capital Train. This trip on the train was a new and exciting experience. We were able to go to the White House and as well as the Capital building. I do not remember all of the specifics but do remember the ride and the joy of having this opportunity. I did not mention it earlier, but we took the bus to and from the convention from Mississippi. The drive was a realization of the size and scope of our eastern part of our country. I have sketches in my mind of the various mountain ranges and the cities that we traveled through. I do not remember what our food supply was on our travels while riding all of that distance on the bus and train. But, have a keen remembrance of the restaurant foods that we were introduced to. The experience was really funny because we did not have a clue about what we were able to do. We were quick learners and with help from the waiters, along with observing those diners around us, we ended up being rather savvy in our participation at the elite restaurant. I remember how my experiences in Home Economics helped me to navigate the correct etiquette for ordering and using silverware in a five star restaurant. We were able to do this on a couple of occasions as well as the formal functions that we were privileged to attend. There was an award banquet and a dinner where we were recognized for our bravery in the Jackson Library Sit-in. I remember well, the auto coin operated restaurants that I used more for most meals because they fit my budget. The foods from the coin restaurants were good and the hotel restaurant was great. Before this encounter in the library my opportunity to travel or to eat in a *restaurant* was limited if not at all. We may have eaten out of the back of the bus station or even a sandwich made in a juke joint but did not have a real restaurant experience.

My limited first trip was from Vidalia to Orange and back as a little girl. We drove there with a family member and returned on the bus. I remembered this trip well because we were in the back of the bus on a long stretch and was entertained by white teens singing, "She'll be coming around the mountain when she comes". They sang every verse and probably added more for the long time that they sang. It was the first time that I heard this song and it was interesting. They sang it so long and so much, it was penned in my brain with words, tune and all. I visualized the horses and the red pajamas as the song was sang long, loud and joyously.

Once I moved to Mississippi, I went on a high school senior trip to Alabama before going to Tougaloo College. There were short trips with the athletic teams that I traveled around Adams County and Wilkinson County to the south of Natchez. My participation was as a member of the marching band as a majorette. As you can see being in Philadelphia was a major trip for me.

While in Philadelphia, I was in a new city and environment but I was comfortable because the majority of us had the same desires and goals for our future. This scenario gave me hope after the agony I experienced from the library sit-in. I got the feeling of freedom as I sat in those restaurants and ate without any hassle and with the pleasant stay in the hotel. Philadelphia was the historical place where the Liberty Bell is famous. The city uses the Liberty Bell as a tourist spot and draw visitors to see it. Everywhere there were stands and loads of little bells were sold as souvenirs. I made sure that I always have a Liberty Bell in my procession as a reminder of what and why I walked into that Library in Jackson, Mississippi. It was my symbol of Freedom. For our country the

Liberty Bell means freedom for all citizens. So for me, I capitalize on the Liberty Bell because it represented freedom for all citizens. The bell also represented our rights to even attend the National NAACP Convention. The Liberty Bell represented freedom that Blacks now experience! I acknowledge that freedom is not free, and that it comes at a cost of giving up something, whether liberty or life. All citizens are given a constitutional mandate to be free to live in this society with Liberty and Justice for All! This freedom is not always appreciated by many today. Because of the life I lived and the experiences I have had, I appreciate every opportunity given to me. It is my desire that citizens of today learn the sacrifices that were made by so many in order to make this freedom a reality. Today, as I live and breathe, I am sharing my story with you but it is really for my children and their children. I am not selfish so I will say that this freedom is just what Dr. Martin Luther King said when he spoke so eloquently in a speech, about freedom for all human kind.

During the summer I was chosen to go to Washington, DC to give a talk on our involvement in the March 27th Sit-in. It was my very first airplane trip and I had to fly out of the airport in Jackson, Mississippi. This trip was initiated, sponsored and facilitated in conjunction with the Mississippi NAACP of which Medgar Evers was the field director. When I tried to board the plane and take my seat next to an older white woman, she refused to sit in the seat with me. A compassionate white man took her seat and helped me endure my first time flying. His presence calmed me in that very hostile situation in the beginning of the trip. My flying was accomplished successfully and I was met by a representative of the sponsoring organization and carried to my hotel. I was treated very well on this occasion as I represented by sharing my experience in the Tougaloo Nine Library Sit-in. I was escorted back to my hotel and my meal was at an interior café. This was when I learned very early to be aware of kind men who looked for unsuspecting young single travelers. I evaded this trap and was able to enjoy my stay at the hotel before leaving for Jackson the next morning. My entire trip was a success and I was met at the airport when I returned by Medgar Evers who saw to me getting back to Tougaloo College campus.

I was now attending my second summer of classes in my scheduled plan of three years and three summers. Medgar facilitated the entire trip and my being able to represent Mississippi. He picked me up and saw to me getting to the airport at the onset of the trip, as well as the facilitation of the trip in the first place. I had no personal expenses but do not remember getting an honorarium either. By my being in school, I was delighted to be given the opportunity to have an airplane flight. I was honored to be sponsored and allowed to again visit Washington, DC. Medgar Evers was a wonderful, supportive individual who also gave his life in the end for the cause of social injustice! I want you to know that his work and life was not in vain. His efforts and ideals are in infinity as a museum in Jackson, Mississippi. Because you and others are reading my story, you also can see that Medgar Evers was a very important participant of the Tougaloo Experience. He was a pillar of support in civil disobedience resulting in the integration of the state of Mississippi.

Chapter 16

History, Events, Risks and Change taken by the Nine.

During the time right after World War II people left the south where *Cotton was King* because the money earned was not much more than being a beggar. A decent living for families took making a change for better wages or even a salary. I had to take the steps that I took to make a difference in my financial situation. My family comfort zones changed and with some great risks. Working in the cotton fields was the only way to make a living at one time. My granddad had it better than most of his family when I was old enough to understand how it all worked. My dad and his family had another choice of work but it was grueling and dangerous. These next money producers were in the saw mills where Dad worked as a young man. He did this before I was born, but I got to see the strain and damage this work took on other men in the community at an early age. Men who were still young in age looked old very early in their lives. This is what I was able to see because of all the cousins that did this type of work in the town of Ferriday, Louisiana. Sawmill work was not only hard work, but was very dangerous work. Many who stayed in the small southern towns had to depend on the only money making that they could. Granddad Alfred was blessed because he did not have to work in the saw mills.

Granddad was a Forman for a plantation and land owners. He drove a truck back in the 40's which was a unique job for a black man. He owned his own land and home, but his brothers lived on land owned by Cotton growers. They worked the land as Share Croppers. Living in the homes on land provided by the landowners held each of my granddads' brothers and other workers accountable to the landowner. Granddad drove the truck to get his brothers and the workers to the field. After the landowner, there were the sharecroppers, tenant farmers and farm laborers. The last three job descriptions of workers were a step above many of the part time laborers who only worked when the crops were in need of maintenance or should I say, designated unskilled workers? However, the entire system was designed to keep the blacks in another form of slavery. There were no labor unions for the farm laborers at that time. The landowners were rich and super rich because the system that they used left, my relatives and blacks to feel the brunt of this way of life. In 1948, my relatives were still living under those low paying work systems! It was in the 1950s that I noticed this way of life starting to decline.

My cousins and many of the younger generations that I knew moved to the north. Some in the neighborhoods began to go to college. By the 1960s the median income for blacks in Mississippi was estimated to be around $1,500.00 a year. The income for Mississippi Whites was about three times higher according to documented reports. The differences in income whether from farm work, factory or saw mill was always much lower for blacks than for whites. I know a lot of this for certain because of the habit of listening in on the conversations while the grown folks talked, sitting on the front porches of Vidalia, Louisiana and even in Natchez, Mississippi.

Black women in my community worked as day workers, cleaning homes for one or more than one family but regardless the standard wage was $3.00 a day flat. Aunt Carrie worked for the mayor of Natchez, made the standard wage working almost every day. Her perks were better, which increased her bring home financial worth. Meat and food items were often sent home because the Mayor and most whites only ate what was cooked each day. Because of white families not eating left-over's the workers got to take the food home to their families. Day workers, like my Aunt did not have to purchase the food and it was cooked at the employer's home, taken home ready to serve their families. This was a way of life that was still going on even in the Jackson, Mississippi area while I was a student at Tougaloo. My roommate convinced me to work on a Saturday for her so that she could make a special meeting on campus. I did her the favor for that one day. I got the one sandwich, a glass of water, a full day of cleaning, ironing and was driven back to the campus in the backseat of the car with $3.00 in my hand. That was the very last time I did that!

The event of the Tougaloo Nine Sit-In in Jackson, Mississippi started something that in my estimation took on a life of its own. The event changed the playing field for employment and the ability to earn a better living for black citizens in Mississippi. What happened in Jackson was relegated as the *Eye of the Storm.* The term became known as an icon of the era. (internet n.d.) There was turbulence in the area around the start of this civil rights movement made by the Tougaloo Nine.

I remember going into Jackson for various meetings and sometimes stayed overnight at the home of dedicated supporters. There were events held at individuals' homes and other meeting places. There was also an air of caution because of the unknown responses of the white community regarding our continued meetings to make a change. There was something in the attitude of blacks that was to turn the state of Mississippi and the entire south into a frustrated and yet satisfying reality. It just depended on your tolerance for the change and state of mind for acceptance. This emotional and physical struggle led to a change in many areas as is widely documented!

My hometown Natchez, was always considered, *Old Money*. Compared to the Delta area, and cotton fields of Louisiana the Miss-Lou area had money to work with from other sources. Natchez started out with the large Plantations which are restored on an ongoing basis. But that did not mean prosperity for the black citizens. The area in the 60's was ripe with new factories, which started with the end of the World War II. There was the new International Paper Mill, The Armstrong Tire Factory, the Box Mill and the Pecan Factory which hired mostly women. In our family both Uncle Alfred and Dad got hired at the International Paper Mill. Our neighbor next door worked at the Pecan Factory, which was seasonal received a better income than most women that I knew.

Natchez is filled with soft timber and forests of Pine trees, giving some blacks the opportunity to join in the well paying pulpwood industry. This was possible because families owned land acreage with timber growth. Many blacks combined as family enterprises and brought their own trucks or rigs. Some blacks were able to cut timber from their own family owned acreage. This land was not used for cotton, which was king in some counties. Pine trees would point to the sky and scent the air with its fragrance in Adams County where Natchez is the County Seat. Because of the climate other soft wood trees grew very fast in the Adams and Wilkerson Counties along the Mississippi River across from Louisiana. All of this area surrounds the many old plantations, which now are on the antebellum home tours.

When the new factories, opened black men had a better chance at making livable wages for their families. This is what balanced the scales of economics before the end of segregation for black families. Compared to the old wages dependent primarily on field work blacks now had new opportunities in the new factories. Now blacks were able to live a better life. With the new factories came unions and union pay. Blacks had the more menial jobs in the factories as documented by the job my dad was able to secure. Blacks now had better paying jobs than ever in their history, for the greater majority of them.

There were very few jobs as supervisors in the field work like the truck driving work that was done by Granddad Alfred. My granddad was a rarity in that era. The lack of good paying jobs in the vicinity of the Miss-Lou area was the major reason my dad left Vidalia to go to Orange, Texas in the first place. He went to Orange because of the oil fields and it was not steady work. The work was transient and workers had to follow the continued building of oil fields. The blacks were used as unskilled laborers and dismissed when they finished building the facilities. The whites were hired to work the oil rigs as skilled workers. My dad returned to the area of Natchez, Vidalia and Ferriday, Louisiana when he learned of the classes for Veterans held in Ferriday, Louisiana. The factories were also being built and Uncle Alfred got hired in the building stages of the International Paper Mill. He shared this information with Dad who was later hired for some of the outside work with the wood on the wood lot.

This was the area where the logs are watered down continually to keep them alive for the use to make the pulp. Those logs can remain usable for years after being cut down by keeping them well watered. Dad found favor in this work. He endured the weather and found ways to be relieved because it was not as demanding as some of the work he experienced as a younger man.

This factory work increased the wages and living status of many blacks in the Miss-Lou area. The old money continued the ongoing preservation of the pre-civil war period. This concept continues to prosper and thrive in my home town and the vicinity around the bend of the Mississippi River across from Louisiana.

The ongoing Annual Pilgrimage of Antebellum Homes that I enlightened you about earlier in the chapter was lucrative for the area. This industry brought tourist to Adams County and kept the pre-civil war period alive even today. The Pilgrimage was a slap in the face for many blacks because citizens were hired just to reenact the slavery scenario. This was degrading but was one of the ways many blacks could depend on employment for some months during the year in the pre-Integration era. It was similar to the cannery work that is seasonal work in California. You did not have a continued job but could look to be hired during the tourist season. However, there were no unions and set pay scale for those who worked the tourist season of the Pilgrimage. Besides, if you were not working in the Pilgrimage you could not just visit any of the antebellum homes. Those stately homes were not for the blacks to enjoy or be a part of on an ongoing basis. They were only for staging the blacks as players in the enactment of a bygone era. The tours of the antebellum homes were situated all over the Adams County and Wilkinson County to the South. Today, there are two seasonal tours and the riverboats with hotels built just to accommodate the tourist. This industry has blossomed but it was always a part of the old southern pride. There never was any shame in this industry by those who profited from it. Today it is more historical and lucrative yet wields that status at the expense and exploration of the black citizens. Jackson, Mississippi as the capital and major hub of commerce, in my estimation should have been held accountable for the repression and degraded plight of the conditions, *Black Citizens* endured for so many years in all of Mississippi. However, that was just the way it was until the "read-in" by the Nine in the Jackson white-only library. The opening of Mississippi with integration that was started by the Tougaloo Nine rippled over all areas of commerce. There are those who may disagree with me. However, history supports my rationale. As integration was being applied, many black businesses were lost. At the same time blacks were able to be employed in industry and commerce, as they never were before. This beginning of integration had such an opportunity for economical growth afforded to Blacks. But, in order to enjoy this opportunity blacks had to continue their education to get this benefit. If blacks did not attend school and get an education, they still were not welcomed into the retail stores with the same acceptance of whites even with only a high school education.

The Freedom Movement in the South was targeted to the most hard core, oppressive and segregated states of which Mississippi was said to be in a class by itself. Now, this is the historical *fact*. The governor of Mississippi in 1961 was Ross Barnett. He was the one who had all of the Freedom Riders put in prison. May God bless his mean spirited self? What do you think? I really pray that he repented for his hatred and harsh dealings with so many blacks and others who came to Mississippi to make a change. He along with many others did not want to have a change in the demented thinking of white citizens during that era. He demonstrated the callous disregard for anyone who breeched the oppressive segregated state imposed laws concerning the unjust practice. Mississippians prided themselves as the purest of segregation. For us, the blacks, *colored* there were imposed on us, the three absolutes: racism, violence and poverty.

It is for this reason that I shared with you that Natchez was more *urban* in that there was no cotton fields and because of its place on the Mississippi River was good for shipping. Adams County was and still is pulp wood country. Many blacks made a substantial living in the wooded hills and forest area around the county. Yet, the area was just as repressive as other parts of the state. The aftermath of the library sit-in only validated the prejudices.

One year, during the break between regular school and summer school, I ventured to the Natchez Employment Office for a job. I was refused a job even after giving my vitals. They had my current classes and experiences of which I had quite a few from working in my aunt's store. I was told that I was overqualified. That phrase is what is known as a cop-out. They did not want to hire me or even suggest the possibility of hiring me for anything other than what was normally *reserved for coloreds*. That was an accepted fact because I experienced this mentality. For simple clerk jobs at that very same time, young white high school girls were working. They worked the checkout stands at our local Newberry, Five and Ten Store, and even JC Penney's. They were your typical high school students and probably recent graduates, yet they qualified. They qualified because of the color of their skin and the cultural as well as racial connections to those who were behind the employment office desks. There was no one working at those desks that looked like me!

Before I left the employment office, I was asked if I could cook. Now, the assumption was always that *blacks could cook*. It seemed that a local Board and Care facility a few blocks away called and asked for a cook. My take on the matter was that the cook did not come in. Without a cook and perhaps they were there with raw and fresh food that needed to be prepared for Lunch. I relented in part because I was interested in seeing what this offer really entailed. I can say without any reservation or bias that the facts of my summation of the job search was true. I went over to the address and was shown into the kitchen. It was the worst cooking area I know of anyone's in my family circle, but that is not the point. I had a large fish that I baked, cooked side dishes and perhaps even bread or a cake. I had to wash the dishes and prepare for their supper before I left. When I did leave, I was handed $3.00. As you may guess, I did not return. Nor did

I want to cook for $3.00 a day in a board and care home as my career. What that experience did for me was to solidify my desire and goal to finish my education and have a real career in the educational field.

The segregated education for blacks was severely limited as a choice made by the educational politicians. This was evident to me as a high school student in a new school in the mid 50's when we received *new* used books from the white high school. Clearly, the McLaren led Adams County school district did not spend 50% of the school budget on the black school. I do not have statistics on that number, but common sense and mathematic says that to have an equal number they have to match. Now who is fooled by the *separate but equal* school when the numbers were so one sided? If the blacks got the five year old books from the white school, I would say in five years the books got their full usage and were ready to be discarded. That would make the numbers more unequal than ever. I would say that the school supplies only cost the district the fee for delivering the books to the black school. The whites had 100 percent utilization of the funds set aside for educational materials. It was a good thing for the black students to have Historical Black Colleges and the few Black Community Colleges that were available for black citizens. Tougaloo College is one of those Historical Black Private Christian Based Colleges.

If black students finished high school in the Natchez area, finances was a big situation that needed a solution. A college education was the way to overcome in the South but it was not an easy task either. We were not all full scholarship blessed. Thankful some of us made it on work-study and student loans along with minimum scholarships and hard pressed minimum family support. Higher education was one of the ways blacks escaped the continued poverty and menial jobs cycle. Many of my classmates started families early with only day work and unskilled labor as a compensation choice.

Overall, Mississippi was still economically and politically dominated by plantation owners. In the meantime antebellum homes and vast land holdings of soft woods cut as pulp for the paper mills dot the state. Where the *Old Money* mentality and financial reality come from was established earlier. Mississippi has many banks and they are financial institutions with great holdings. We simply call it, *Old Money* because it has been around for a long time. There was vast wealth in the South and even after the civil war many families retained this wealth. They may have gained this wealth because of the way the constitutional laws governing land holdings and the workforce fueled by poor and primarily black workers. Senator James Eastland was in office during the era of Tougaloo Nine and pre-segregation period which was also called, *the Eye of the Storm*. (web Links, Mississippi, The eye of the Storm n.d.)

Senator Eastland led by example by also being a holder of economical riches while using the system that kept the black in a depressed living situation. What I want you to know is that the depressive life style is what I referred to when I told you about all of my granddads brothers who lived on the land and sharecropped out a meager living and still could not get ahead. They were put off of the land when the owners sold it for residential development and the blacks could not even afford to, if they could live there again.

In 1961, the time of our historical Tougaloo Nine Library Sit-In another example of the Senator's huge plantation was the large profits he made off the cotton crops. His profits would have been in the millions today after paying cotton pickers, $3.00 for a hundred pounds of cotton and get this, $3.00 a day for hoeing the cotton. From documentation, Senator Eastland would have paid black men, women and children who labored in his fields for up to 10 hours a day about 30 cents an hour. Only those who could pick more than a hundred or two made more for picking the cotton. Let me take you back to Ferriday, Louisiana. When my husband and his family worked in the fields during the 50's his mother could pick up to 300 pounds of cotton a day. The children together would pick perhaps up to a hundred all together. It was no surprise because at the time Mrs. Hollis was separated from Mr. Hollis and as a single parent was paying for her own home. Yes, she was a homeowner, and took care of her eight children. She did not collect welfare or general assistance. She did not claim hardship or a disability. Besides, there was not any welfare in place. What there was in place was neighbor helping neighbors, hard work, doing without and using natural resources to survive. There were those black citizens who knew how to use their best skills and labor to their advantage.

Now back to the dialog about the situation documented in history regarding the Senator Eastland of Mississippi. Those employed to work this cotton crop of plowing, planting, hoeing and picking most likely were black men, women, and children. The cotton area was primarily in the Delta area of Mississippi. My first experience in the Mississippi Delta was when I did my Supervised Student Teaching to complete my Educational Teaching Certificate.

When I did my student teaching in Hollandale, Mississippi in July 1962, the school sessions for the black citizens were staggered so that the blacks could work the cotton fields. I have a chapter set aside for those details. But I must share those details in order for you to see how and why black citizens needed the state opened for Justice. I share some of the history of what was the acceptable way of life for citizens in general. Now, I ask you to also remember that very much all of what I am sharing with you is from my memory from fifty years ago. Much of what I am writing come to me as I close my eyes and just look back to what was and remember why I wanted you to know what I experienced. My explanation is to let your mind follow me as I remember and feel the agony of my family, blacks in general as they etched out a meager living yet maintained a rich culture. Ask yourself the same questions I ask and if you like, see what you come up with. A good example of what I am trying so hard to get you to see is the next question. How was it possible that not only white citizens but also the State Senator reaped the riches of the land on the backs of the blacks and without any repercussions? I was appalled at the split school sessions to accommodate the blacks working the fields yet, this was the only place I found to do my student teaching in the summer session. I did what I had to do and understood the premise from which the blacks endured their way of life. They simply did what they had to do to work out a way to make a living under the circumstances for their families.

You may have heard the term, Jim Crow. Well this is the economical and social system that Mississippi was famous for and I lived those times. I saw and experienced the degradation of using the Black citizens for wealth without any of the benefits or wages offered to the White citizens in similar jobs. Black citizens were under this system for many years of agricultural feudalism by State Constitutional Laws. If you are confused or not familiar with the term feudalism let me give you the definition of the word. As a noun, it is the economic, political, or social system which began in Medieval Europe. The land was worked by those who did not own it but was bound to it. The people worked the land in exchange for services given by the overlord. Senator Eastland owned vast land holdings and he had workers committed to working his land, first because they lived on the land. They did not pay to live there perhaps and in fact owed the senator allegiance. They earned very little to nothing for their work. At the end of the crops season as it was with my granddads brothers, they had little or no resources for another year. They usually were allowed to put everything that they consumed all year on a tab and credited to an account that the white network owned and operated by the landowners and proprietors of the businesses. The workers could never get caught up and did not if ever at all get a balanced account. In my thinking, this was just another form of slavery. Look out consumers, Today, you are finding yourselves in the same situation. It has been said many times before, if you do not know your history, you are destined to repeat it. Beware! Black folk and people in general, understand that you cannot out spend or live to the max with this kind of financial mentality. The landowners are like the credit inducers of today. You can easily get caught in their web and even remain there for a while. They bide their time because what you do not know is that you cannot easily get out alone. You are destined just as the sharecroppers, the cotton pickers, the hoers of the landowner's crops while living on their land.

It was a fact that the structure of the state laws repressed the blacks. The whites terrorized the blacks with the use of *systematic disenfranchisement as revealed in the event* that coined the term, *Eye of the Storm*. Blacks were in the web of economic downward spiral. (Web Links, Direct Action n.d.) The blacks were a casualty of the life that was put upon them and they had no law or compassion from anyone because it was all about the money. Did you get that? It was the same with slavery . . . It was for the economical state of being. It was all about the money. Old money, new money, no money or repressed ability to have money was what made this a fact. It was and still is all about the money. What the change in the law did was to allow the blacks to escape the web that had been woven around so tightly by the fact that individuals and even the senator was able to work their acts of compassion to help the blacks by allowing them the opportunity to live on their land, work for penitence and live just at ground level. The blacks had no choice but to accept this ideal. The blacks did not have a voice in the political arena in Mississippi. The blacks had no voice in their communities. The blacks had no alternative for their life. Life in this status, of *poverty* for the blacks was accepted from the poorest land owners, to the *State Senator*. In order to keep many blacks from revolting or protesting, the threat of jail was used while the KKK was used and allowed to threaten or kill blacks. Meanwhile decent white citizens turned their heads in denial of this ongoing depressive lifestyle. Some may have done so because of ignorance or simple because it was a way of life for them. Who knows what is was then? However, after the change of tide by the integration of the Tougaloo Nine, whites, blacks and all races saw that they were capable of living and letting others live to the best of their ability.

Despite the attitudes of Mississippians about the financial and economical status of blacks, adequate jobs and employment was the key. This was shown when the International Paper mill moved into Natchez. Mississippi's economical changes came slowly, because changing the way you lived depended on the money you had to live on. Health and nutrition also depended on the ability to adequately feed the family.

The most reliable sources of self-sustainment came from the small home gardens that most black families depended upon. When I grew up in Vidalia, before moving to Natchez, there was always a garden and neighbors who shared their bountiful crops. This was not the case when we moved to Ray Street. Again, we must acknowledge that as the economical climate improved there were better jobs but not the same access to healthy food items. One item that I want to share with you is that there were foods that were grown and shared with families like our large family. The vegetable was called, something like Cushaw. It was from the squash family and was as large as a watermelon. It was versatile and could be cooked like candied yams or stewed. My family always graciously accepted any that was given to us. When I look back, it was like, *Manna from Heaven.* There were large grocery stores in town and none in the black residential areas. However, in every block, there was a front room store where black citizens sold sundries and some processed meat like baloney, salami and cheese along with crackers, cookies and perhaps chips. They also sold all kinds of penny candies and sodas in glass bottles. There was no deposit on the drinks purchased but when you returned a bottle you were given a penny. Sodas were 6 cents and if you brought in six bottles, you could get your drink *free.* I realized this was a way to get the sodas free and so did the other children in the neighborhood. Every young person understood that their proactive participation in their refreshment was beneficial. It was like, on the job training for your future financial status. The reality for me was that I can state emphatically that the wounds of the economics and commerce were slow to heal. However, citizen's black and white experienced revitalization because 50 years ago, nine young students from a little known college took the risk to make a difference.

Part 6: Voting Rights!

Chapter 17

Voting was a Challenge under Suppression,
Not a Right!

I was not aware of all of the political juggling going around our beginnings of desegregation of Mississippi. But I do know that we started something that would bring change. The aftermath of the start of segregation by the Jackson Library Sit-in and the Tougaloo Nine deeply affected the voting rights agenda in Mississippi. Change is a vital part of life for all living elements. The sky, the earth, the living things in the sea and on the earth as well as the highest living form that God created is constantly changing. But during the Jim Crow era, the whites did not want the blacks to change. Blacks were supposed to live content with the status quo of being domicile and at the same time content. Black citizens or humankind was not at all able to think and desire as is evident in all things living are driven to desire, grow, learn, know and succeed. Can you comprehend this blatant suppression of the *Black Citizens* in these United States of America? Remember this mindset was in the timeframe between the World War II and 1961, when I participated in a civil disobedience to change the dominant mindset of the white citizens in the state of Mississippi. Do not let your guard down because today there is still racial profiling. Because of the change, blacks can now vote. This is a constitutional right. But to be right, the vote of every citizen has to be exercised! One of the main reasons for the civil rights struggle was to give everyone the opportunity to vote.

I was a part of this change agent for justice and freedom for all mankind, black and white, the *Tougaloo Nine*. What I did at that time is a part of who I am, what I did at that time gave men, women, boys and girls the opportunity to live their lives with the right to vote without the Poll Tax and intimidating oral questions asked in order to*, pass the exam to vote*. The change in mindset of the white citizens opened the federal constitutional laws up for people of color and mankind in general to have the opportunity to use the laws and constitution to register and vote the same as any other citizen in the state of Mississippi and the United States of America. Citizens of Mississippi were and are citizens of the United States!!! However, the state of Mississippi envisioned being more than the constitution of the United States of America. The State of Mississippi was the Sovereignty State of Mississippi, with a commission to suppress the black citizens and relegate them as less than citizens, not my belief but their documented rights at that time.

After the Tougaloo Nine opened the door for civil disobedience, the Freedom Riders came to the south to document the racism and show their support for getting the mentality of superiority by whites turned around. Three young men lost their lives in this display of support. It was discovered that the southern white power structure was more violent than first imagined. The whites opposed the black's right to vote much more than their right to desegregate lunch counters, libraries and bus stations. The project to get blacks to register and vote filled the news stories with brutality, bombings and murders as they were attacked by the Klan and white citizen's councils bend on keeping this superior arena for themselves. Many blacks tried and wanted to vote but were discouraged by the brutal tactics used by those white groups. When individuals, such as young black adults, educated individuals did make the effort to try to vote, humiliation was used.

It was the custom at the time to intimidate the Black Population so that they were discouraged from registering to vote. I experienced this for myself and I have a firm mental grasp that this truly was the tactic. I remember how I went down to my local Voter Registration office in Natchez, Mississippi in 1959 after my 18th birthday. I was asked by a young and not very informed young white lady to answer verbal questions that may or may not be correct. It was the custom at the time to intimidate the Black Population so that they were discouraged from registering to vote. I lived through the events and went into the process to obtain this knowledge for myself. I as a result of my action I know that this truly was the tactic. There was also a *Poll Tax* that had to be paid twice if I remember correctly in order to just register to vote. They used as many deterrents as possible to dissuade the *Coloreds* as we were called from being in the position to Vote. We needed the law to change, because the white citizens did not want or need the law to change. To change would give a larger group of unwanted individuals, blacks the right to make waves and decisions that the whites presently were in total control of. The question to be answered here is why would they want to make a change and lose their superiority? Now you may be able to see the rationale but this was not right for blacks and citizens of the United States of America. So, it was that "The Voter Education Project Act of 1961—1968" made a difference, although with some Controversy. (Web Links, Voter Registration n.d.) The change did not just happen. There were marches, sit-ins and even death to get to the constitutional change.

As I have acknowledged, the white citizens did not want the blacks to have the right to vote and made it very difficult for us to do so. By the way I am one of the ones who made waves to make a change and yes, I embraced the right for all citizens to vote.

There were more black citizens than white citizens in rural Mississippi yet they were prevented from voting. The establishment used the same tactic that I personally experienced and it was successful for those who were and let themselves be intimidated by this method. This and similar tactics kept the white in control of all of the public laws, maintaining white supremacy with ruthless strategies. The rigged *literacy* tests and Poll taxes were used on the blacks during primaries, and were successful in keeping the local public offices with white only citizens. Arrests and economic retaliations were all used to keep blacks from the Voting Polls. By the 1961, Historical Jackson Library Sit-In, there were less than 10 percent of blacks registered to vote. Remember, there were more black citizens than whites in many of the areas, but they were not allowed the right to vote.

My dad was a military veteran as was my uncle and many others, who endured the war. Those soldiers endured the degradation as they observed their friends and families being denied this constitutional right. Many black soldiers died for this country and others were denied the right to register and vote for the state or United States political representatives. Now, that is what we know as suppression and the desire of those who wanted to be supreme. This inflated ego was at the cost of labeling and treating black individuals as being second class citizens. It was not just the color of our skin, but education, economics and yes, the right granted by the constitution to all citizens. History proves this because it was only after the Voter Education Project in Mississippi, that there was an influx of black citizens being elected to public positions all over the state of Mississippi. In fact, if you will allow me to comment here, I want you to know that although the blacks were elected to offices in great numbers, they were still humiliated. Many local black political officers, mainly mayors of small towns followed some of the same procedures as their predecessors in the same manner that the previous white mayors. Many of the white mayors handled the financial reins in such a fashion as to give favors to certain businesses, neighbors and friends! When the blacks followed the same strategies, they were voted out of office or simply, recalled. Yes, this may not be entirely factual but is entirely true that once the blacks got the vote by the larger number of black citizens, they were still dismissed by quorum of dissenters for so called infractions.

Do you really want to know why the Tougaloo Nine Students risked life, liberty and their freedom to cross the civil rights divide that was held from us for so long? There was discontent and a desire to have the pinnacle of freedom, the determination to vote our choice of political candidate. Do not be alarmed but this systematic denial of Black voting rights was the same in the other border states of Louisiana, Alabama, Georgia, and South

Carolina. Mississippi was more blatant and determined to remain superior in political and finances. As I have tried to enlighten you already, Mississippi was not ready to give up this *suppressive constitutional stronghold* that they held over the *black citizens*. But it was destined to change from the suppression the white citizens applied. With intervention and opening up the state of Mississippians' actions against the black citizens, they had to recognize that voting was a right, not just a choice!

What I did was most unusual at that time March 27, 1961. Unusual because there were nine students who felt the same inclination that I felt. We were change agent for justice and freedom for all mankind, black and white. What I did at that time is a part of who I am, what I did at that time gave men, women, boys and girls the opportunity to live their lives. To have the right to vote without the Poll Tax and intimidating oral questions or rigged literacy tests to, *pass the exam to vote*. The State of Mississippi was in for a Voter Education and citizenship change for progress and fairness for all citizens!

Fifty years has passed, with the right and expectation to vote by all citizens, determined to take this privilege seriously nationwide. Personally, my life was on the line for this right. So many other caring and compassionate individuals did the same. In fact, many lost their lives to make this disservice known to the nation and to get it changed. The Jackson movement and the ensuing Freedom Riders gave life, liberty and spent time in jail also for this privilege in Mississippi. Young People of all ages have and continue to be awakened to the struggle which was made so that all men and women could have a voice in this democratic process. Somehow and in many ways the reason for the struggle has been lost on many black citizens and other young adults, in personal and self serving agendas. Frankly, the most dominant reason, so many do not take this right seriously, is because they really do not know from whence they came. They do not know their own history, because it has not been taught to them. The schools have not been teaching it but the first teachers are the parents and even they may not *know* their history. The freedom to vote remains a right. What a positive result because of the civil rights movement has been documented for those who understand and use this right wisely. Citizens you have been given the right to vote, use it at every opportunity. Someone took tremendous risks in order for this to happen. It has been proven that if you fail to know your history, you are destined to repeat it!!!

Part 7:
The Results of Tougaloo Civil Disobedience on My Career in Mississippi

Chapter 18

Student Teaching and Life Lessons

The First Summer Session

In life and all that you do, you have residue, results, consequences or even rewards. The results of my studies at Tougaloo College were not at all exciting for me when I got to the final summer. For one thing, I was exhausted, somewhat frustrated and my parents were just about out of money. I was also engaged and expected to be married to a fellow that I met at the 1961 NAACP Convention. Yes, I dealt with all of that and no I did not share this information until now. My mother was still having some complications from her breast cancer operation on her left arm where they took the lymph nodes out. The arm continued to swell. She did not let this interfere with living each day to the fullest as she always taught me.

Money was tight and but my mom wanted to go to the National Baptist Convention which was to be held somewhere in the south. I shared with them that I was just fine. It was something that I wanted to see my mom and dad have the opportunity to enjoy. So, I pretended that I did not need any more money and let them know that the amount that they agreed to pay was all that I needed. I shared somewhere earlier that I almost passed out due to mal-nutrition, because I had no extra money, dining privileges and no roommate to help support extra needs that last summer session on campus. I was in a dorm room alone with my studies and only my suitcase of canned goods to subsist on.

My mom believed me when I said that I did not need any extra money, after all she had no reason not to believe me. I never let her down or misled her that she knew of before. We would always talk things over but I kept this quiet so that they could make plans to go to the National Baptist Convention. My dad was a pastor and she was a missionary. She wanted to go on this trip and I wanted her to go. She deserved to go. She had no outlet for recreation and vacations were not a part of her lifestyle. Her youngest son was around eight and could go to Ferriday to spend a week at Aunt Lucille's Place.

We all took turns working in her small family business when we were there in Ferriday, Louisiana. We all got time to go there each summer for as long as I can remember. So my Mom could to attend the conference along with Dad. Mom made herself a new wardrobe with sleeves to cover her arms which were appropriate for a missionary of the church. She made about seven beautiful outfits in all.

I went back to the college after spending a week with the family. I had major decisions to make. I did not want to get married before the summer was over which was the plan. I did not want to have to marry and leave my mother right after, I completed my requirements. I did not want to go to Illinois where my fiancé and his family lived. His plan was to continue school, working on his masters degree while I worked as a teacher. The plan was to have the wedding and leave for Illinois all within the same breathe. Because I was not ready to make that choice I told him, "no". I said "we could postpone the date and do it at another time". He said, "No, if we could not get married then when we had the time that we would not get married". I said, "Okay". I cancelled all of the plans. My next response was to burn the decorations, napkins and all of those things that had been supplied by Aunt Leanna and Uncle Roscoe. Both of them were looking forward to being a part of the celebration. They were always first and ready to support me in all celebrations. I continued to work towards getting my student teaching done the next session. My goal was to finish my course work and get my student teaching in place for the successful completion of my degree in Health and Physical Education.

There was something else in the mix. There were rumors that we may not be allowed to do our student teaching. Dr. Shannon who was responsible for Supervised Student Teaching and placement was adamant in pursuing our cause for placement. He found us a place in Hollandale Mississippi. This was in the Delta Area of Mississippi and had a unique school system and could accommodate the students from Tougaloo Christian College as we were known then. I was delighted and ready to make the commitment. I was so very much interested in finishing my requirements and start my life as a teacher of physical education in Mississippi. Not Illinois as my ex-fiancé had planned for me.

The Hollandale Experience

Upon finally leaving Tougaloo after the first part of the summer session, I went back to Natchez to take the remainder of my personal belongs. You may be able to draw your own conclusion at this time and be correct. I was finished with all credits and would not be coming back to the campus for any more classes. All credits were finished for the degree in Health and Physical Education. My Student Teaching experience would give me the credit that was needed to earn my Mississippi Teaching Credential. After the student teaching I would receive my teaching credential in the mail. My trip back to Natchez with all of my processions collected from the three years of attendance at Tougaloo Christian College was one of profound pride. Yet there was sadness to leave the hallowed halls of excellent academia, as well as the memory of the Tougaloo Nine unforgettable experience!

My stay in Natchez was very brief, yet apprehensive. My personal funds were just about zero. I asked my parents for the sum of $50.00. Remember, this was in addition to the concurring payment of $100.00 of one month. I knew that this would be a strain for them, but they were good stewards of their finances, which is where I got my basics. Upon receiving the requested $50.00, I promised them that I would give them the money back when I returned. I did not know how or when I would do this but this was what I promised. This was what I was determined to do. I took the Trailways Bus to Hollandale and called the principal of the high school when I got to the bus station. This procedure was already set up for all students from Tougaloo College by Dr. Shannon. So with determination, my two Samsonite Luggage pieces and the coveted $50.00 along with a few dollars I had in my procession I made the contact. The principal picked me up, carried me to the school until the end of the day and then proceeded to take me to the home where I was assigned to stay for the endurance of the six weeks of student teaching.

I was the second person to arrive at the private home and chose to stay in the front room of the house. Two other young ladies came and one ended up being my roommate. We were all required to pay around $15.00 a week for our rooms. There was a fee of $10.00 per week each for meals. The landlady did not seem interested in cooking for us she simply told us her prices. I paid my room fee and thought about the proposal. Since I got to the home earlier, I walked around the small area and found out what was available. I did not take long to find this information out. The main three businesses that got my attention was the bank, the grocery store and the movie theater with the entrance for *colored* to the balcony. I opened a bank account at the bank and established a checking account with them.

That $50.00 that I got from my parents was the seed to start being an independent young adult. It was from this presence of mind that I formulated the finances in my head. With my experiences for managing, cooking, and preparing meals, the plan was easily set in motion. I added the $40.00 the four of us would pay to the landlady for food. It was a no brainer for me to talk with the others about my plan. They had only to give me the money and I would provide the two meals that the landlady would cook for us. I would also provide snacks and lunch to take to school. Did I tell you how hot it was there in Hollandale? Did I just share with you that I would shop for food, carry it to the house and cook it every day for all four of us? Well, that was what I did! There was only one stipulation. I would not wash dishes. The young ladies, agreed to clean up for the duration of the six weeks dividing the task between them.

We also had to hand wash our clothes, iron them, walk to the school and back. We had to make meetings after school and attend any night time school activity. Yet, in spite of all of those school responsibilities, I chose to take care of all of the food. To begin, I collected each of their $10.00 and they were willing to do as we agreed. I must have been mighty convincing. With the $30.00 that I collected from the young ladies, I paid the landlady $15.00 each week and was able to use less than the $15.00 left to purchase food, and essentials to make the three meals with snacks. This included sodas and a flavored powder mixed with water and sugar. It was a traditional drink enjoyed by all in a glass of ice on those hot sultry Mississippi Delta days.

Finding Students to Teach

The Student Teaching Component in Hollandale was a great advantage for me. The split session worked out well for me. When July 1962 found me successfully finished with all of my academic work, I was happy to have a place to practice my supervised teaching. I was grateful to have Hollandale as a place to participate in Supervised Student Teaching.

There were several Physical Education Majors. Only one was needed for each gender, because boys and girls were taught separately, by genders during those days. One worked with the boys and the other with the girls. I was left without a supervising teacher, but was allowed to use my creativity to design an

Elementary Physical Education Program in the Elementary wing of the school. There were six grades and five days. I visited every grade level and every teacher. I talked with them and found their strong points for Physical Education. For many of the teachers, this curriculum knowledge was very limited. Many of the teachers were of the mindset of letting the students out just so that they could get a break. Based on their needs, I designed the amount of support for their grade and class. The older grades were given sports skills and game activity using as close to possible the correct equipment on hand. There was no concept of mine to bring along bulky and heavy playing equipment to work the children. It was usually the schools that supplied balls and implements as well as provided for playground accommodations. My job was to provide the playing games rules and regulations with adequate warm-ups and exercises for each ability level. The students were excited for this totally different way to be out of the classroom and proved it by being very cooperative. Each class was taken out with the assistance of the teacher who stayed for the duration in the beginning. Soon they saw how well the classes progressed and began to give me full responsibility. I had no problem with this. The goal I wanted to accomplish set the guidelines for a modified Elementary Physical Education Program.

For the younger children, I designed activities and lead-up games using the accustomed playground balls. The emphases were on traditional learning skills for each group. To set the learning expectations students had to learn the precursor for any learning environment. The specifics taught were; listening, following directions and cooperation. From this fundamental groundwork, movement was introduced. The classes were given locomotors movements including the basics such as: walk, run, skip, hop, jump, slide or side step on grass. To teach them non-locomotors movements we made modifications to include: bending, stretching, lunging, balancing and push-ups. One of the activities that provided them so much fun was in using manipulative movements. This component included using small objects which taught each to reach their interest in unsupervised play. They were introduced as well to a combination of movements with and without equipment. The major equipment was the large playground balls used for recess. This was a valuable lesson, because it challenged me to be professional and at the same time work with the teachers in a way to guide them into understanding how to continue offering a fundamental elementary Physical Education Program as a part of their classroom experience after I left the school. The session of Elementary Physical Education as an assignment was noticed and commented on as very positive by our Tougaloo Teacher Education Supervisor, Dr. Shannon. This was a very wonderful feeling of accomplishment. This session became not just a great recreational activity with students but a good teaching experience. I was and still am grateful for the opportunity and experience at the school complex in Hollandale, MS.

When I returned to Natchez after my six weeks of Student Teaching, I returned with my processions, my experience under my belt and the promised $50.00 for my parents. I also had more money in my purse than was there before I began the six week stay in Hollandale.

This is what I later learned about our placement of student teaching. It was this new information that let me know that it was more than my personality or skills that made my summer of student teaching a successful participation. I was able to finish all my requirements in my planned program only by the grace of God. What I learned was that, Graduate Teacher Education Students of Tougaloo had limitations. *"We had even more difficulty when we tried to place our students [in schools to do student teaching]; those who were going into teacher education. Placing them into schools where they could do their student teaching. Placing them where they could get full employment because some of the school districts would not hire Tougaloo students; for fear of those students bringing their political views to the district and disrupting the system."* (Web Links,digital Library-Tougaloo College n.d.) This article was a part of the digital library on the Tougaloo Nine. It was my opinion that this quote would give you a clearer understanding of the impact our actions on March 27, 1961 made on me, my co-participants and the whole Tougaloo College student body.

As a result of this mentality towards us during the early sixties, I felt it both in student teaching and employment. As a teacher, I was limited to only a couple of localities. In reality it was just one! The only place that I could do my student teaching was in Hollandale, Mississippi. It was Cotton Country. This was still the Jim Crow Era. The split economy was set-up so that the blacks had school in the summer months before the cotton had to be picked. The white schools were on a standard schedule. Blacks were scheduled so that they were out of school during the cotton picking season. Continued degradation in the school system with facilitation to use the blacks for laborers enhanced this revered economy. This mentality favored the white landowners and was not easily stopped.

My Hollandale Journal

During the six weeks that I stayed in Hollandale, I was able to maximize a living skill that has been a thread of connectivity in my lifetime. I will tell you what I remember of the experience because I did not write it in my journal. My journal was strictly about the recreation and lack of it during my stay. As I shared with you already that my stay was in a private home with three other young female student teachers.

It was at this very time that, as a young adult I had the presence of mind to journal my stay in Hollandale, Mississippi. Now remember, I was 19 years old at that time. This was my evaluation of the place and time I found myself in. Certainly time, experiences and appreciation for the citizens, especially the *Blacks* may have changed in those last 50 years. I gave myself credit for having the presence of mind to journal my feelings in part, if not in more detail. The total experience may have been too much for your eyes to see. Being truthful means leaving some things to your imagination. Read along with me as I share my journal with you.

Recreation: Between the Cotton Rows by Geraldine Edwards, 1962

"Here in the heart of Mississippi, in the Delta, famous for its cotton, lays a little town called Hollandale. There are several stores, mostly grocery stores and they do have a Health Department and a City Hall. They also have a Police Department with one Negro officer.

My main concern is with the Negros recreation, but I can't help observing the Whites' recreation also. In doing this I have observed some of their unique characteristics of living.Here on East Crouch I share with three other Young Ladies, a private home. There isn't a daily Newspaper as such but we get first hand news from our landlady. Everything that happens is her concern.

The School has a Student Council and Teacher Committees but it is an autocratic place run by the principal. He makes the rules and he enforces them.

My first couple of weeks found me in faculty meetings approximately four days out of five. There was no formal meeting and the occasion was simply anything the principal had on his mind—or for insurance cookware salesmen or simply a letter from his son.

Someone wrote the principal a letter, telling him about the only recreational activities the young teachers have. Truthfully speaking the writer degraded the teachers. When I arrived here in July I was told not to frequent the small cafes and dives here in Hollandale . . . But when I saw them, I had no desire to do so. There was a semi-nice place that was used for recreation in Leland about 20 miles away. However, after this particular letter, the principal called a meeting and asked us not to go there either.

Most of the young teachers live in a Teachers' Home. They have a room where they can play cards but I saw no other facilities for nice wholesome recreation. In the place where I live, there is a Television which is broken and we aren't allowed to play cards because the neighbors may talk. So most of us have nothing for recreation except the balcony of the Movie Theater; which is almost unbearable and (Thank God) we have reading. There is simply no where to go to give us an outlet. By the way there is no public library where we can find nice cultured or even educational books. The two Drug Stores do not have an adequate supply of novels! So is our fate?

We wash, we iron, we cook, we eat, we go to school and we teach. We joke and maybe we read or just sit and talk in the evening. At any rate, our life is at a stand—still. We end up repeating our selves day after day. The weekends can be better or they can be worst. Most of the younger set goes to Jackson; those who do this have a better weekend. Those of us who remains here can't do much other that sleep, eat and sleep. We have the worst of the weekends.

A walk could help, but that is almost impossible. The weather is terribly hot here and mosquitoes are as large as house flies. They get about equally as well, night or day. Besides, it doesn't take but a couple of minutes to walk all over the town. Drives can be enjoyable if you can stand to look at cotton or rice for miles and miles. There isn't anything worth looking at except the dirt and filth.

The teenagers are no better off. For social recreation without much drinking, they frequent the Hall and the Kitchen. These are cafes with jukeboxes where the kids can dance. You can always find some teenager fellows on the streets, all the time. They drink, smoke, curse and just about anything kids in their situation will do. They have a few vacant lots where they play game similar to baseball or softball. They use a stick and a soft rubber ball from the ten cent store.

The church helps serve them as some recreation. They have programs and regular meetings; sometimes they even have church suppers. That person of families whose sole income is from the cotton crops gets less recreation than anyone else. They hoe and pick cotton from dawn to dusk and are so tired afterwards that they usually go to bed after the evening meal.

The school is deeply concerned in this Delta way of life in a negative way. Some students come to school at the beginning of the summer session to be registered and they may come to school once a week until it rains. They all come to school on rainy days because the fields are wet and they can't work. There is what's call the split-session school. The summer session is from July to September; and the fall and winter session from October or November to May. The reason for the split-session is to enable the Negros to plant and gather their crops. The whites didn't have this split-session. Many of the Whites own the land or can work in the few stores. Some even own the stores."

Now, I want to take you back to the Journaling and the student teaching which all of this chapter is all about. However, since, I have opened up myself for you to see, it was expedient that you see the connection of my financial applications during the years of the manuscript, Back to Mississippi.

Years have passed; society has caught up with this same mentality for many urban and ghetto communities. This thought is only opened because, in spite of the sacrifice and risk of the Tougaloo Nine there was still pockets of society that did not get the message that someone paid a price for them to have a better life. Although there were opportunities for more, the mentality has seemed to digress rather than improve for a more positive lifestyle and living life fit and well, mentally and physically.

Now, here is another example of the teaching opportunity after the episode of the non-violent civil disobedient Jackson Library Sit-in.

Chapter 19

My First Teaching Job

After my successful student teaching experience, I went home to Natchez in order to sort out things in my mind and to get my finances in order. Remember, I brought my parents the $50 back after the experience there in Hollandale. So, after being finished with my requirements I needed a job. I needed to get my priorities and finances in order. I knew what I wanted and what I now needed. I would be looking for a job in Mississippi, Louisiana, or preferable the Miss-Lou area. I did not get any information before I left for student teaching on school districts and had to go with what I knew to research for the position and places. Yes, in order to do justify my education I needed to earn some money. *Being a student who recently, finished all of my requirements for graduation did not make me a, graduate.* I could not dwell on this fact, because my present task at that time was to get all of the paperwork in order. Since leaving the campus I had to work independently on securing placements. I was able to get the information for all of the school districts around the Miss-Lou Area. This information was expanded upon to include districts up to 50 miles away from home in all directions. So I began to send out applications, for a job in Physical Education. My major in Health and Physical Education also helped me to have a double minor, Biological Sciences and Mathematics. I did not include searches for my minor areas at that time. As time moved on without any success, I sent out letters with all of my information. It was around the winter break when I got a response that was a possibility. This was a long time to wait but I used the time constructively, reacquainting myself with neighbors, friends and the community schools.

Upon hearing from the principal of the farthest town in Mississippi from my town of Natchez, I was elated and welcomed the opportunity. Natchez is on the Mississippi River side of the state to the west. Meridian is on the east side of the state towards the state of Alabama.

My interview was set for the spring break which was about a month away. When the time came, I was ready. Off to Meridian, I went for an interview with the principal of Harris Jr. College. I did not drive and had to travel from the west border of Mississippi to the east border which was a day's ride on the bus. I was able to get the principal to secure my housing for two nights in order to arrive on a day and prepare for my interview on the next day, spend the next night and head back home. All of this was arranged for one week in the spring. The interview happened. I had enough time to see the city, the school and all their facilities. A Physical Education teacher was on maternity leave during the year. Another teacher was needed to meet the growth of the school. So the school would need yet another teacher of high school Physical Education for the coming school year. The principal was in charge of the high school and the junior college staffs. Have you heard of compromises? Do not get me wrong but understand that I was a young lady and had a responsibility to fulfill. I was willing to leave home to go to unfamiliar surroundings to start my career. You will be surprised at the politics and personal restraints that had to be juggled in order to feel comfortable in this new community. Despite the pay scale, the placement, the work expectations of all teachers, it was received as a true blessing.

There was no such thing as a teachers' union. You had to negotiate for yourself. But count it all good, without challenges, there would be no justifiable raw success. I got the job, which would start as a Teacher of Physical Education for the next school term. While I was still in Meridian, I had the opportunity to see the tremendous Harris Junior College, High School and Junior High School Complex all on one campus. The principal I was hired by was directly over the complex, but was the principal of both the junior college and high school. There was a junior high school on the same campus with a different principal. The gymnasium was used for all students, junior college, high school and junior high students. There was an exercise and dance room as well. There were the girls and boys, separate facilities and an athletic department. It was a huge complex.

Since I was given a letter of acceptance for the job, I was free to volunteer at the junior high school back in Natchez where my younger brother attended. It was very satisfying to be around boys and girls even as a volunteer and to get an idea of what I would have to be aware of. One of my most memorable duties was to build a float for the PTA of the Prince Street Elementary School, of which my mother was the president at the time. To get more experience in teaching dance to younger children, I started working with them at the North Pine Street Recreational Center.

Since it was no charge to me, the lessons to the children were at no charge, but I gladly received donations from those who wanted to give. I was amazed that I survived for almost a year without any salary, but I did. One of the character traits that I learned early in my life was to give to others, using my time, talents and influence. Although I did not get a salary for all those months, I was able to be sustained by the grace of God and was able to live at home and enjoy my parents for a little longer because I stayed with them at the home on Ray Street. It was a blessing that was given to me because I had no inkling of what the future health of my mom would be. I also chose to have my diploma mailed to me, due in part to not wanting to take more finances from my parents. I did not march across the stage with the class of '63 because in my mind and mindset, I was of the class of '62. My take on the matter: Why worry about something as small as a number of the class you graduated with? No matter, what I think, you can find me in the class of 1963. So in reality, no matter the class distinction, I am one of the members of the Tougaloo Nine. Of that I am certain.

About a month before summer school was to start, I was contacted again by the principal of Harris Jr. College. He wanted to hire me for the summer to teach Mathematics to junior college students. These students were mostly athletes who were going to be on campus for trainings and were able to take classes while there. Athletics was very important to the school and many of the athletes were put in summer school classes to get some of their credits before they had to play sports. This was just fine with me. However, for this job I again needed a loan from my parents. I promised to pay them back when I was paid. This was a very good feeling. I enjoyed the fact that I got a chance to work in a field that I enjoyed. I would to be able to familiarize myself with the facilities and the community better. The summer session was six weeks. I was able to rent a room with the family that I stayed with for the two nights during my Job interview. Miss Snowden was a secretary at the junior high school and was instrumental in helping me adjust to the job and transition of living as a new teacher. I chose to rent the room and provide my own food. I did not do very well this time, with the food due to the long distance to the grocery store. Miss Snowden felt sorry for me and often invited me to eat a meal on Sunday with her family. It was a very good summer. The students that I taught were young men mostly and were just two years or less than I was. This was the hardest part of the job. I had to teach these young men a serious subject and whenever, many of them got the chance, they were asking for a date! I remained professional, and made the summer earning my first check for $ 500.00.

Before I returned home to Natchez, at the end of the summer school session of teaching, I found another place to stay for the long term. It was a room with a family for $35.00 a month with meals. That was the going rate for teachers, for many who lived in private homes. For the summer, I paid rent and brought my own food. This did not work out too well as I shared with you earlier. I have to acknowledge this fact that I did not eat as well as I should have. So, with the Davis Family, I chose the board and rent option. I got a better deal than I knew at the beginning when I first made this decision. Mrs. Davis worked in the cafeteria which provided lunches for all students and staff from all three schools. Mr. Davis owned a café with his mother and from time to time I helped them out with serving and waiting tables. It all worked out in my favor.

The beginning salary of my first full year work, I was paid a total of $3,250.00 for the year. I was so proud and knew that I could make it on that amount of money. I was just happy to have a job teaching Physical Education to high school girls in Meridian. I shared how I only made 500.00 for the summer's work when I brought my summer school check home. I had to set positive seeds for my brothers so I cashed it and spread the money on my mom's bed. All of my brothers looked at the money with awe; they sighed, and were hooked. My brother, Pete who was debating on going to the military or take a partial athletic scholarship to Mississippi Valley State, made his choice at that time. He was reassured as I assured him that I would help him as our parents had helped me.

The first thing that I did with my money from the summer's work was to open a checking and savings account at the bank. With my mom's help I established credit at the Singer Sewing Machine Company store. Here is where I purchased my first very own sewing machine. This was my first furniture also. I carried the sewing machine along with me to Meridian. My new wardrobe was made before I left Natchez, along with my professional Physical Education White outfits for class. I was ready by August when school started with the help of my dad who drove me to Meridian with my wardrobe and new sewing machine. I was ready to go to work.

Although there was segregation of the school facilities and teaching, one of the strong points of the city's Physical Education

Program was the workshops and shared equipment. The units were scheduled between all schools and all major equipment was rotated to the schools no matter the race, black or white. The workshops were informational for instruction and safety. Demonstrations were made for all equipment and handbooks for each teaching unit was shared with all teachers, but only at a separate time for white and colored! The Director was white and worked with each group of teachers. The instructions were given at the white school and some follow-up were done at the Harris complex. This was especially true for the trampolines. Stunts and tumbling were among the units that used the mats, balance beams and vaults with safety instructions. Dance was a big unit with instructions for the variety of dances taught. One of the best parts about this Physical Educational District Wide Program was the workshops for every change in mid-semester and units. Remember, ladies taught the girls and men taught the boys in most of the units. For dance and track and field we co-taught. It was a very good experience and I benefited greatly as an individual and as an, informed teacher. When I moved to California, I brought my Meridian Physical Education Handbooks and my professional membership in the Alliance for Health, Physical Education, and Dance with me. This was the National organization; the California Professional Membership was added after I moved to California. The California organization was named, California Association for Physical Education, Recreation and Dance.

Because of my experiences in Mississippi, in the early 1960's I was open to allowing boys to participate in my classes of junior high school physical education in the early 1970's before Title Nine was implemented. The boys asked to be in my class and upon an agreement with the male teacher in charge; we allowed a few of the boys to come to my class for instructions and participation. They went back to the boy's side of the gym for shower and dismissal. They were not allowed in the office which was in close proximity of the girl's restroom and shower room. No co-ed was accepted in that area or era.

Part 8:
You cannot escape all the changes in Life's Journey.

Chapter 20

Some things are Major Distractions

For all of my life experiences, up to and after the Jackson Library Sit-in my mom was the center of my stability. She grounded me and at the same time she molded me to be the individual I became. I was allowed to make my decisions at an early age. My mom gave me the tools of meeting my challenges face to face and to be responsible for my choices. When I decided to ride or skate while in Vidalia it was a risk of being in a place not acceptable or even one of bodily harm. True to my character, I chose to do them any way. When I decided to be a part of the Tougaloo Nine group and participate in civil disobedience I made a choice without really knowing the consequences. I knew the history of similar consequences in other southern states where black students sat-in at the *lunch counters*. I still took the opportunity to be involved. In my short life span at the time I really enjoyed opening doors to new ventures and to go where no one in my extended family ever dreamed of making a reality.

It was never before planned by me to open the doors to the Jackson white-only Library. This was not on my schedule or agenda when I first walked on the sidewalks of the Tougaloo Southern Christian College in September 1959. The times that I grew up in, were those of segregation. There was *Jim Crow* compliance of suppression and rampant corrupt practices against blacks. The ideology of the white citizens was to keep blacks and other people from attempting some of the things, which I did. Many blacks went along with this ideology as a way of life. Adults were quick to tell young adults to not rock the boat. They would use other colloquial terms such as, this is the way it has always been. The reality is that people were not comfortable making a scene or being identified as a scene maker. There were regulations in place such as harassment, jail or putting the word out that you were a trouble maker. Trouble makers were designated as such and were easily picked up by the local police as a suspect for any infraction. Our parents always taught us to respect the laws even though we did not agree with them.

People did not risk their lives and reputation with the law or their back side as I did when I skated or biked around the town of Vidalia, Louisiana. When I ventured into the neighborhood as a young black girl of seven, I did so with no fear. Yes, I was aware of the attitude, belief and thinking that *Blacks or Negros* should be lesser individuals to them. Not just a name or design of character but as an entity. We were not supposed to have that kind of freedom. But regardless, I chose to venture as I did in the white neighborhoods. We lived in a small town and there were no interactions of blacks and whites, even the children. My mom knew my attitude in being proactive in doing activities and she knew that I would be a child, yet she was my major supporter. Mom encouraged me to do things that I wanted to do by preparing me to meet obstacles. After we moved to Orange, Texas I was only four years old and she allowed me to attend Sunday school alone. My mom had a young baby and she could not go with me.

She knew that I wanted to go and attend. She told me what to say, what to look for and how to behave myself. She watched me go alone across an acre of land to get to the front of the church. I walked to the church and participated in the services after which, I returned back to the tent in which we lived at that time. I proudly brought my card home with me to share with my mom what I learned.

We were able to obtain a small unit in the new projects that were built to house the growing veterans and their families. She taught me by taking me there and back on how to safely go to the rental office from where we lived. I walked for up to five blocks alone with the $25.00 each month to pay the rent. I made sure that I got the receipt for my mom. This is how she taught me and what I was expected to do. I followed my mom's instructions and did the same procedure each time. The clerks in the rental office would quiz me on why or how I could at my young age of five and six years old do that task. It was an easy task for me because my mom demonstrated what I was to do. If I followed her instructions I would do the task and not be afraid. My mom depended on me to be responsible. I did what I had to do to help out because my mom could not do it all. I walked to school alone in the first grade also. Mom was pregnant again and could not walk and carry my baby brother. My mom knew me and my capabilities. I was just fine once I learned the route. I was always a responsible girl for what my mom needed me to do. Don't get me wrong, I was quite mischievous and also loved a good challenge at an early age. Not only did I love a good challenge, but I would fight if I was provoked or mistreated by the other children.

Earlier, in another chapter, I shared how I promised my mom that I would take care of my Brother Pete's college expenses. This was a responsibility that I took on to ease the financial burden on my parents and to give back as they gave to me. It was at this time that I formulated that if each of us Edwards would reach out and help the next one in college we would all be okay. So let's get back to my mom's plan.

When things like fees and tuition came due for Pete, she would contact me by phone. Sometimes she would let me know in one of her weekly letters. She simply let me know how much and when to pay. I always took care of this by going to the nearest money gram store to get what was needed and mailed it without hesitation. Money grams were much more acceptable and guaranteed at that time. I was dedicated to following up on my part. I knew how important it was to know that I had my mom and dad's support for the three years and three summers that I attended Tougaloo.

I went to college on the fast track and did not miss a beat or any social interaction except one. I pledged AKA and became Ivy. However, due to time, money and especially my academic schedule, I did not follow through on this. At heart I am of that AKA mindset, I just did not fulfill the commitment. It just so happened that the colors for the sorority were my favorite colors. Remember my first room decorations were pink organza. My first teen birthday party colors were green. Both colors of green and pink and their shades always were my favorite colors, and they still are. Of course it was not just the colors that intrigued me. It was the personality of the sisters. They were more studious and had an air of sophistication about them that I related to. That was a whim, because I found that I am all of those characteristics all by myself. My mom was the most interesting of any friend I may have had. She was always candid with me in finances and life, as I became a young woman.

Because letter writing was the most economical way to communicate my mom wrote to me weekly from the onset of my college days and up to this time we are now discussing. A lot was revealed by my mom's letters. She would always talk about most things happening and kept me updated on all of the family even after the cancer. I should have known that something was not right. She complained of not being able to see the lines and apologized for such a sloppy letter one week in November of 1963. She always wrote my letters she sent to me in green ink. My mother had no problems letting me know that she loved me and that she was proud of me. I was her oldest child and her only girl.

By this time in life she had five boys. The youngest was only nine years old and such a big baby. He got to spend a lot of time with my mom in his developing years. Mom was always at the school in a volunteer position and working with the PTA. Volunteerism is something that I too, have always made as a way of giving back to society. To volunteer as a young lady with the Natchez Northern Community Center with boys and girls in dance was one of my first stints of volunteering as an adult.

My mom was occupied daily in gas sales, fixing hotdogs and hamburgers as she maintained the small family business along with my second brother, John. When I count back, John was only

15 and made his 16th birthday on November 20, three days before my mother made her birthday of 41 young years. At the time my brother, who was old enough to drive was helpful in getting the other boys around to games and school affairs and appointments. Dad worked, at the International Paper Company, where he had been employed for twelve years. My dad led the congregation as the pastor and was a supporter of all of the sports and activities that the boys were in. I was away from home working for my first year as a teacher of physical education. I was so very happy and blessed to have that job. My search for a job had taken a long time and went all over Mississippi and Louisiana. Since, I was working I supported my brother Pete with his finances. I came home for Thanksgiving of that year and did a double celebration, in theory because we also celebrated my mom's 41st birthday. Thanksgiving was the third Thursday of November and her birthday was just a few days prior on the 23rd. She looked tired but I assumed that it was because of the work at the business and also the cold weather that made the concrete flooring much colder. I was concerned but was so very interested in making a good impression because Meridian, Mississippi was the only job offer that I got. I did not focus on my mom but do remember her looking tired. Whenever I was home I would always cook or help with the majority of the cooking. I helped out but was preparing to get back to my new job and in my mind wanted to be the best I could at my job. I am sure that I felt that I had to justify my work because I was appreciative of the only offer that I really got.

I cannot be sure but I do believe that the job search was not because of my resume. I felt that I did not get any hearing from any other district for another reason. I know that my name was associated with the civil disobedience event that I was involved in. Through it all I felt honored to be able help my family in my new position and this was rewarding. I wanted to be as supportive as possible. My main goal, was to help because my family has been so supportive in spite of the risk that I put them all in.

Much to my ignorance at the time my mom was not well and her sister Leanna came to get her. I did not know that she was as ill as she was. My aunt lived in New Orleans and believed in something that I found objectionable. She used all kind of weird mixtures and concoctions. A good example was to sprinkle salt all around her bed. She brought ammonia by the quarts and used it in her bedroom for something. I loved my aunt but she was sometimes very unpredictable. At any rate, she let my dad know on around December 13th that he should come and get my mom. My brother John drove because my dad was distraught. He found my mom in a lot of pain and it was on a Tuesday night that he got her home and called me. My dad called me when he got back to Natchez, Mississippi. From what and how he said what he said, I knew that I had to leave for home immediately. I left Meridian Wednesday on a Grey Hound Bus and got into Natchez to be in the hospital with my mom that evening. I stayed all night that Wednesday night. She was in so much pain, she tried to keep quiet but her pain was too intense. After my dad called and before I left Meridian, Mississippi I cried all that night. I am not one to easily cry and have found myself only crying when it is the worst of situations. When I cried, I meant that I absolutely wailed. I cried myself dry, in the end I was just dry sobbing. I had no more tears to shed. I did not cry any more until months later when the reality of losing my mom really set in. I did not cry during the time I spent with my mom or after she passed.

The Thursday morning that she passed, she asked me to go home and rest. She knew that I had come from Meridian and spent the night with her. I agreed to leave only when the nurse said that she would clean her up. *There was a very strong smell of urine.* I wanted to clean her myself because I felt that the nurses were not taking good care of her.

At that time in my life, I felt the segregation and lack of care that so many blacks experienced during that era. I felt that my mom did not receive the best care. She did not seem to be dying when I saw her in the hospital. My brother John was devastated and he blamed the hospital for somehow being negligent. We could not justify why my mom was sick unto death. She was young, vibrant and she had a lot of life to live. She had a lot of love yet to give. No, it was too soon for her to leave us. The hospital was a general hospital, with the majority of the hospital devoted to other citizens. For the blacks there was a wing on the right side of the hospital that may have previously been a sunroom. It was in this small space that all blacks were cared for in. One side was for men and the other for women. No matter the condition, all blacks were housed in this little space which constituted about 10% of the total hospital space. I was there all of that time and they did very little to make her comfortable. I told my mom that I was going to JC Penney's to buy her a new robe to wear. She smiled, in spite of the pain she was in. I left with the intentions of going home for a short rest after buying the robe.

When I called the hospital to check on my mom in just over an hour, I was told that my mother had died. My mom had just made 41 years old on November 23th. The time of her death was just over a week before Christmas. My mother was gone and we did not know why. She had survived breast cancer, chemo and x-rays. She was finally able to enjoy life and experience her dreams of having her daughter being a teacher and her oldest son in Mississippi Valley State College as a football player. She had the small family business and she had all of her children in school. For as long as I could remember, there was always a baby or toddler in the house. My mom and I was at a place in life where we could communicate as adults and she was proud of that fact and I was proud to be in that place and time in my life. I was angry, hurt and confused but I had to be strong for the rest of the family.

That day and the next was the beginning of a fog, I never before experienced. I was walking but not sure which way I was going. For me this state of being was most unusual. For the first time in my life, I was not sure of myself or really why I had to make the choices that had to be made. It had to be done and I was groomed to take care of situations in our family. Because it came natural, I was the one to make the decisions. My dad was a wreck! As an adult I understood his pain. He was just a young man himself with four boys at home, and his love, his companion, the mother of his children was gone. He also did not know what happened. Neither did I. But we had to meet the situation as we found it and make the results work for the proper procedure. It was difficult and I had to do it all. My mom leaving me was a real major distraction in my life plan.

When I was in my second year at Tougaloo, I had a dream so vivid that I woke up crying and wracking with heart breaking tears. There were three of us in the dorm room at the time. When my roommates asked what was wrong. *I was never one to cry . . . hardly ever!* I shared with them at that time that I dreamed that my brother Pete who was the second oldest, died while he was away in college and I had to call my mom to let her know. I was so overcome with that dream that I had to share it with my mom. She comforted me and as usual reassured me that everything would be alright. Well, in December 1963, my brother Pete was at Mississippi Valley State College and I had to call him to let him know that our mom had died. Somehow Pete got home the next day.

We planned the Home going for December 23 of 1963, and it was snowing in the Miss-Lou area. My grandmother, Mama Tex was living in Ferriday, LA with my dad's sister Lucille, because my granddad died a few years back and my aunt Leanna did not want her to live in the family home anymore. My mother's younger sister lived there with her three children and she was both married and separated from her husband. Almost all of the family lived in Louisiana across the Mississippi River. The snow made the bridge almost unusable. My grandmother and aunts, cousins and other relatives somehow made it to the funeral and it was a sober occasion. The entire repast was taken care of by church members and neighbors. The repast was in our home adding more to the soberness. I tried to return some of the utensils and dishes before I left for Meridian. It was next to impossible. This was another heavy fog in my life. I do know that mom was buried in the snow on the side of the fence in the Natchez

National Memorial Cemetery. Coping with adversity is one thing, taking charge when everything and everybody is immobilized is a challenge that I was not ready to tackle. This part of my sharing is to document that inner strength is best known when it is called and relied on in an emergency or life-changing event. All of my life experiences did not in any form or fashion prepared me for this death, and especially under the circumstances. You see, my mom was diagnosed as having cirrhosis of the liver.

Mom did not drink or smoke. We were torn because we suspected foul play or toxins. But how and when did she get the toxins. Questions still plague me in what, when and why it all happened the way that it did. My mom was just barely 41 years of age when she died. When I got to the age of 41, I had a phobia that was hard to shake. I suffered from anxiety and my blood pressure soared. I had to take medication for both. My system went through many symptoms during those years. Unfortunately this was just another challenge that I had to overcome.

This time and event were a big distraction but the distractions continued. The next day after the funeral and burial of my mom was Christmas Eve. I was saddened for my brother David. My younger brother was just a little boy nine years old and we wanted to get him a game or something for Christmas. There was not much to choose from and we were not of a jolly mind to do much shopping. People were kind and gave their condolences, but there was not the kind of outreach that some today extend. Because we waited so late, we were offered games that were display items or even missing parts. This did not ease our feeling of being denied joy or happiness. My baby brother benefited from the time he spent with our mother more than the rest of us. He saw all and he used the best from all that he observed to make his life what my mom would be pleased with. Distractions in life may be painful but the recovery is in the knowledge that our mom was truly a great mother to all of us. For me she is always in my memory. This has been so hard to share. It is to help and it is her legacy to all who come after her, me being the best benefactor.

We are grateful that we knew the real reason for the season that Christmas. Yet, our hearts were heavy. We just lost the one who kept us all together. I owe much in the form of attitude and fortitude to Mom who was the motivator, the tradition keeper, the one who knew what everyone needed and sometimes wanted. She was the one who made everything festive. She gave, she supported, she encouraged, she hugged, she was full of laughter, and she made fun of things to get us to laugh. Mom knew her daughter and she scoped and knew each one of her sons. My mom had a plan outlined for each one of us. She knew all of our weaknesses and she knew all of our strengths.

My mom was my hero. She was the second girl in her family and the one who was innovative. She was the one who initiated the remodel of the family home in Vidalia, Louisiana. She was the one that had bathrooms put in the home in Vidalia where this saga began for the first time. The house was divided into two units to rent out one to support the remodeling so that my younger aunt could remain in the home without any financial struggle. Aunt Christine was handicapped at an early age and the home was given to her because she needed it to be so. My mom was all of these things to all of us. To my dad she was his everything.

I turned the death into a more cohesive obligation, by coming home often. I still did not own a car and took the bus, the reliable, still sitting in the back because some things are hard to change.

When my mom died, my dad was lost. I was so worried about him. He continued to work and to preach. He continued to be a dad and he learned to cook. He never had to do these things before. But learn he did. He personalized everything, as pop's biscuits, pop's chicken fried the first time without flour or a coating. I showed him how to do this and he could have challenged the secret herbs guy. My brothers all learned how to wash and iron; and take care of getting themselves ready for school. However, running a household was more than that. I left Meridian as often as I could get away on weekends. I missed some classes, but I had to do what I had to do. My mom's death and home going was a big distraction in my life and my psyche.

By summer time we all needed a change. We needed time to come together as a family and heal. So we made plans to go on vacation to none other than, Orange, Texas. This is where my journey in self-realization began by traveling alone at such a young age. We had to come together as a family unit and heal as they all healed when, I put them all at risk as a part of the Tougaloo Nine and the life changing event.

Part 9:
Family, Time to Heal.

Chapter 21

The Vacation

One car, four drivers, seven occupants, six seats, two grocery bags of snacks and the trunk full of clothes to last at least a week. Pete was out of college for the summer, Rev my dad had taken two weeks off from his job on his annual vacation time. All of the boys were ready and I was not working the summer of 1963. We were off to the place where John was born and had no recollection about. Pete the oldest boy was so small when we left he had no memory of it either. We had all kind of relatives in Orange, Texas and we knew just where we would bunk. In fact we stayed with several families while we were there just to get around to as many as we could. It was a real blast.

Most family members lived in the new projects from the earlier years when we were first living there. These were brick two story apartments with all the amenities of the time in each. There were cement stoops and steps for sitting and talking long into the night. There was a clothes line for hanging clothes that were washed and some families even had one of those fancy wringer washing machines. But clotheslines were used as the dryer of choice even without the wringer washers. This was a time when the sun was used almost exclusively to dry clothes. My family, relatives and other black families that we knew also hung their clothes on a line to dry. To top the area off for me were the nice sidewalks to each apartment.

We had the car and being younger adults, drove ourselves around shopping and seeing the town. We brought groceries and snacks and yes, beer in small sample bottles. It was a novelty and we bought into it. Rev was so involved with family that Pete and I, now young adults, were adventurous without his scrutiny. This was our very first real vacation and we were having a good time. Our cousins made sure we did.

So we along with two other carloads of occupants went down to the Gulf of Mexico across Galveston Bay, taking the ferry to Galveston, Island. The ferry to the island was in itself an adventure. Our very first vacation and togetherness found us in the mindset to heal from our new lives without our mom and my dad's best friend.

Here we were on our first trip over to the Island. We parked the cars on the ferry and went up on the deck to watch the waves. On the top deck we were able to view and at the same time dodge the ever present seagulls. The seagulls were dominant on the back of the ferry and looked for riders to throw them tidbits. I laughed at my baby brother David as he tried so hard to lure the seagulls closer to him as he just enjoyed being a boy of nine years of age. The ferry was a great place to do some people watching. In all of our lives, we had never been in a place where there was not a division of races. There was not a *White this* and a *Colored that*. There on the ferry was a better insight into how people could live and enjoy life together. There was no division of where the cars were parked. You parked in line the same as you drove on the highway. We had a new revelation, one that I embraced. I liked how it felt to just be a passenger without having to feel like a second class citizen. My new found feelings of freedom to be an individual was a part of the healing we all felt.

We did have our swimming suits and trunks and were ready to play in the water of the Gulf on the white sands of the Galveston Beach. There were two distinct beaches. There were commercial beaches from the east of town to around Fortieth Street. And farther west was a more soulful, get down beach. The east beach was frequented by younger adults and many with children. There were free play structures and white sand for children to delight in. The beach spans the entire south of Galveston Island and has a very high seawall for protection from the severe weather it has during the hurricane seasons. There is a long drive filled with restaurants, fast foods and vendors who cater to the vacationers. We had choices to eat where we were comfortable and primarily where we could afford. This was wonderful after our history in Mississippi. On the west beach is where we found ourselves. Westward from where we were you could find many young adults and many of them were black. There was constant music of the soulful genre and it was loud and it was danceable. So, everyone came here to have a partying good time. I do mean everyone! There was also a boardwalk. Otis Redding had a hit song, "On the Dock of the Bay" and it played all day! We had a fun time. We played in the water and on the sands with all of the other vacationers. Our vacation was in full swing and our feelings of togetherness were reinforced as we felt in harmony with nature and family. We made our way back to Orange at night again, on the Galveston Island Ferry. We had made family bonds, and memories that would last for many years.

A chance meeting

On our way back home to Natchez from Orange, Texas we stopped in Ferriday, Louisiana. Aunt Lucille's was our usual summer vacation spot every summer, but not all at the same time. There were six of us so the larger brothers went over and helped in the small business. The rest would go on weekends and I would look after my baby brother until I wanted to go out with one of the many cousins who lived on the same street when we used Ferriday as our vacation spot.

My cousin Rosie, Aunt Lucille's only daughter was in a social club, called the Elites and on the night that we returned from Orange, they were having a social in the yard of one of the members. This is the night that my life took a change for what it is today. Everyone was at my aunt's house but being a young lady in my early twenties I drove alone to the social event. One of the guests at the affair was a young man who said that he lived in Galveston, TX. We talked during the entire time I was at the social and he wanted to see me home. I was driving the family car so he wanted to see me safely back to my aunts' home. I drove with him in the car with me to the front of my aunt's house. I stopped the car right out front where we could see and be seen. This was a very important means of being respectful for me and my family. We talked well into the early morning before he walked back over the railroad tracks that divided the black section from the downtown to his mother's home past the downtown. It was a short walk of about a mile by crossing the tracks. But it was the more dangerous path.

What we found out was that we had so much in common. He had a similar upbringing but in a single parent with a strong grandmother. His dad was located in Galveston and was a local black business man. Most assuredly this young man was respectful, determined to be successful in life and he was a Christian young man. He would not tell me his age and I could not tell what it was by looking at him. I did a lot of looking at him. He was a very mature young man and had the values that I found myself attracted to. I later found out that he was a recent high school graduate and was working with his father in his business in Galveston. I gave him my phone contact numbers in both Natchez and Meridian, Mississippi. He promised to be in touch, and he called when he returned to Galveston and talked long distance for long periods which at that time was a big expense. As you may know by now, that young man is the same one I talk about in almost every facet of this developing story, *back to Mississippi*. To you, I call him JH.

JH continued to call me long distance when I went back to work in Meridian, Mississippi. We talked for long periods of time. I told a friend who was the Physical Education teacher for the junior high school about this fellow. Her take was that he was a long shot. I had a fellow in Meridian but he was not what I wanted or needed. During my year of mourning my mother's death I prayed that God would send me a husband. My prayer was for a family man just like my dad. I wanted someone who would love me for a lifetime and who I was dating prior to that time was not that God centered fellow. My casual friend was just a fellow that could be a companion to social events and a ride when it was night leaving school functions which all teachers had to attend. I usually walked every day but accepted rides with him when I could not walk. Yes, I could get the bus and sometimes I did. So this fellow who first and foremost did not attend church was not a priority in my life.

When I look back, I was just biding my time. In the meantime, JH moved to Houston, Texas to obtain a better job. He later moved to California all a part of his plan to better himself. JH and I kept in touch as he moved from place to place. While there in California, his mom let him know that he was drafted into the Army. He chose to volunteer into the Army while in California because he was drafted in Louisiana and could not get there in time. So the Volunteering made a better choice for him. Fortunately, JH did his basic training in Louisiana. We were able to be in touch and eventually planned to get married. He sent me my wedding set of rings in the mail and called to see if I got them safely. It was more than romantic, it was securing his intentions. For me the commitment was an answer to my prayer.

I asked God to send me a husband because, the choice that I had made earlier in my life with engagements and casual relationships did not work out for me. There was trust and a great understanding with JH from the beginning of our relationship. I was definitely headed in a new direction for my life. The vacation made a big difference in our lives because it was healing. For me it was a time to begin to really live the life that I now enjoy.

Part 10:
A New Family Direction

Chapter 22

Married Life!

JH and I had the same values for our life together. We planned a small wedding for family and friends. A friend who had worked with me when I worked in Natchez had been planning her wedding for two years. My friend was intent on having the largest and best wedding in the Miss-Lou area. Her ideal was not at all what I wanted and especially what I needed. All of the memories may not be in exact sequence but they are pasted in my memory as sure as when you read it, you can visualize the occasion from my written words.

While my friend spent her long time planning this elaborate, outstanding, precise in every detail once in a lifetime event, I spent just about three months for the entire process. I had my wedding, honeymoon, and had set up housekeeping from afar off before the time-line it took her to be married.

My friends and family made the wedding ceremony including the preparation, ceremony and reception a glaring success. But it would be sometime later before JH and I would be able to live together as a couple. I continued to live in the arrangement of renting a room in Meridian, Mississippi until after our daughter was born. Moving on with the details of the wedding and celebration is where I want to take you now.

For this very elegant and simple event we had a small group of family and friends. My hostesses were, Aunt Carrie and my best friend from Ray Street, Dorothy. Both Dorothy and I moved into our Ray Street homes with our families in the 1950. We were the first to have girl to girl talk about boys and music and other such stuff. Soon there were two other girls in the neighborhood. We all remained friends but the other two left the area after high school. Dorothy and I remained very close although she was two years older than I was.

My wedding dress was made by one of my friends whose brother was my classmate. Charles was a friend and I did not know his sister until about six months before my engagement. Bertha was her name and she was a topnotch seamstress who did work for many families in the Natchez community. Another friend that I grew to admire in Natchez volunteered to make our wedding cake, because she was a budding baker and wanted to share her talents.

The wedding ceremony was a candle light ceremony which started at 6:00 p.m. with four each of our brothers and who served as ushers. They were all handsome and elegantly dressed in their dark Sunday suits. The ceremony was humorous, because while I was in the dressing room putting on the final touches and getting ready for my dad to walk me down the aisle, I was stunned. Aunt Carrie who was directing the ceremony told me that everyone left the house in all the cars and dad was left at home. There were no cell phones and not even a phone at the church but Aunt Carrie knew the situation. She took action and got a car to go back to the house on Ray Street. We waited while someone went to get my dad. In the while time, my cousin Constance who was also the musician played soft music. Rev was soon there at the church and took his place at the back of the church to escort me down the aisle. Everything went on smoothly from there on. Soon, the ceremony of vows began with the pastor officiating while on crutches. It was not a long ceremony. It was a double ring ceremony despite the fact that JH had taken my wedding band to be sized the week before and forgot to bring it back with him from where he was stationed at that time. Fortunately I had the engagement ring and we used it to complete the ring ceremony. Did I tell you that JH came home almost every weekend if he could make it from the Army Base? Despite the glitches or two, this was a beautiful ceremony.

The reception and honeymoon

The reception was held at the Natchez Recreation Center in North Natchez. This was the same facility in which I volunteered to teach the dance classes. It was a perfect setting for our guests who were mostly family and friends to welcome us as a new couple. After the traditions of cutting the cake, throwing the garter and tossing the bouquet we said goodnight. Our goals were to change clothes and head out for the over 300 miles to Galveston, Texas.

We arrived in Galveston, Texas on the High Island side rather than to wait until the Ferry began to run. Mr. Alonzo Hollis was patiently awaiting our arrival for his part of the celebration. The honeymoon was at a black owned hotel and restaurant on the beach in Galveston. The stay in Galveston was his wedding gift to JH and I. Dad Alonzo always called me Mrs. Hollis and not by my first name. He was very proud of me, not for all of my life experiences, but because he respected me for my life goal and occupation. Someone once said that Alonzo was convinced that I made the perfect mate for JH. After all of the changes that we went through to get to this part of our life we were both so very grateful and blessed as a couple. We both were thankful and in reality knew that we were blessed as a couple and life in general.

Our wedding expenses that I remembered were for the materials for dresses which included the matron of honor, the flower girl and my wedding dress. I purchased my pearls that I wore, gloves, and the flowers for the entire ceremony. The rental of the tuxedos, food, beverages and the wedding photos were paid for by JH. My dad provided the car that we used to go on our honeymoon. The community center was a minimal fee and the church was no charge. Almost everything else was a gift to us. Our wedding party consisted of DeEtter, my dad's wife, JH's little sister, Patricia the flower girl and Duncan who was also from Ferriday, Louisiana. We started off humbly and with minor glitches, yet our lifelong goals were not to make a splash or show. We were humbled because we could not do much better and it was the relationship that mattered most. We are still together and having great times in this same *relationship*. We were blessed for our marriage to be a lifelong strong Christ centered relationship. We continued to have this lifelong goal; to be spiritually centered.

Difficulty within a happy union

Our precious daughter was born premature two months before my due date. I was still employed in Meridian, Mississippi when this surprise happened. She was a breech born baby but I had no long lingering labor. Since, I was still living away from her dad; I had to endure this portion of the experience alone. The Davis family with whom I rented the room during my teaching time in Meridian took me to the hospital. Because she was two months premature she had to stay in the hospital for two months until she reached five pounds. She started at two pounds and ten ounces but lost weight. I watched daily as her ounces slowly moved up. I did not continue to work since I needed to be at the hospital every day. JH was in the army in Texas stationed at Fort Hood by then. I continued to stay at the private home while our baby girl developed. We were financially okay, because I had saved money in order to be able to take off from work from my position which by then was as a counselor. There was no maternity leave and especially no continued pay. I did not expect the long hospitalization but thank God the charges were covered.

It took two long lonely months in the segregated nursery, where she was the only child the majority of the time. I had to confront the nursing staff who kept our baby girl in the white area since there were no other babies in the *colored* area. Every day when I visited, I had to knock on glass doors from inside the colored wing to get their attention to bring my baby to me. There was always a wait because they had other babies to take care in that unit and did not stop to bring me my baby. This upset me, yet I knew that their attention to her was important. My baby needed the human touch and I could not be there but a limited time. So I remained calm for the ultimate development of my baby. I was there as much as the staff allowed me to be. I went to the hospital everyday for those two months. I held her in my arms and cuddled her. She wanted to suck, but was too small to take a bottle. She was fed through a tube that went down to her stomach through her nose. She was so very fragile but I held her close and sometimes gave her the opportunity to satisfy her need just to suckle. There was no milk yet the contact with me was healing for me and soothing for her. It was a long two months. She would gain a few ounces and lose a few in a day or two. I did not know what was happening with her and that caused me to pray so very hard. During all of this time, I did not see a doctor to interact with or ask questions. The nurses were my only contact for information. Thankfully, our baby girl was perfectly formed and had no visible effects of delay other than being so very small. Once she weighed the needed five pounds, I was so happy. I was ready to leave Meridian as I did as soon as I could and did not look back. I was disappointed with the hospital scenario. Surely the hospital staff knew that I was not treated fairly. I was comfortable with the Davis family in Meridian but felt that I needed to be closer to home and to JH. My need was be closer to the Edwards and all of the Hollis family which was in Ferriday Louisiana. It was at this time that I took our baby to Natchez and lived at Ray Street with my dad and his wife DeEtter. We would spend most weekends in Ferriday.

JH and I was the oldest of the children in our families and in both homes. There were still lots of siblings still residing in each home. Natchez had the best set-up for me to stay during this transitional time and I got my old room back which by now was a real room.

The interior of the house had undergone yet another makeover to accommodate the new wife and son that my dad now had. While I was back in Natchez, Mississippi many of my friends and family stated that our baby was not going to make it. She was so very small but she was a survivor. We were determined to do all we could to have a healthy thriving little girl. However, before my baby girl was a week old, my dad and his wife, delivered a baby boy full term. He weighed in at 9 pounds, twenty-one inches long. He was born one week and a day after I delivered my daughter. Moving back to Ray Street turned out to be a bonus for all of us. We were able to pool our resources until the babies were older and we could go back to work.

Settled back in Natchez

The family on Ray Street now consisted of DeEtter and Dad along with my four younger brothers, the new baby, my baby and I. JH was a part when he could get there from Texas. The small family business was no longer in business. However, DeEtter was a teacher of Business Education working in a small town about 30 miles to the North of Natchez. She took off work for about six months before returning to work. She commuted daily back and forth for many years. In fact, she did this until all of my brothers finished high School. Once I returned to Ray Street I began to work after a couple more months at a facility as a counselor which is what I did in Meridian when I experienced the premature birth.

I waited before seeking employment to see my daughter grow stronger and she did improve and began to thrive. Both DeEtter and I pooled our funds together and had a cousin from Ferriday to come and stay in the house there on Ray Street, to look after the babies while we worked.

My new found job was as a counselor in Natchez, MS, working with adults in literacy. In the meantime, JH was stationed in Fort Hood, TX and could come home on some weekends. He drove five hundred miles one way. He really wanted to be with his family. This worked out very well for about six months. When our daughter reached a year old she was potty trained and able to attend a daycare. DeEtter took her baby to Fayette, Mississippi with her daily where her mother took care of the budding toddler.

It was at this time that I found a small apartment two blocks away on Pine Street where JH and I could have more of a family life together when he came home, which was more often now. Coming home to Natchez for JH was always a challenge while he was in Texas but we later worked it out. Rev allowed me to keep the car we used for our honeymoon. I put a new transmission in the family green Pontiac when I moved back home from Meridian. However, before that there was the Grey Hound and Texas Transportation system for JH and me. We would see each other by using the bus system whenever we needed to do so. I would go to see him on base when he worked and could not come home for some time.

One great thing about being on Ray Street was the ongoing support with our baby girl. Weekends were spent in Ferriday with the Hollis Family where our baby girl got loads of attention. While we were at Ray Street we were one big happy family but JH and I need more privacy and time to be a family together. Rev was not pleased that we moved out, but when JH came home on the weekends that he was able to, we now had some family time together and it was a great thing.

My dad eventually became the father of ten and he loved being a family man. I was the oldest and the first girl. The youngest was a girl and there were eight boys of my dad's children in between the two girls, my sister and me. JH and I became our own happy family when we got our very own apartment in Natchez Mississippi. We learned by experience to be very conservative in all that we did. Our first big purchase other than JH's purchase of my wedding rings was our first car.

JH needed transportation to come home and did not want to continue depending on someone else coming towards Natchez or the bus system for me to get over there. So he got a 1965 Pontiac Lemans, in Midnight Blue. We brought furniture, of good quality one piece at a time designed in traditional Maple wood. We paid for each piece of bedroom furniture in full and carried it home to our apartment. When we moved to California, we kept the same furniture style which was traditional Maple. Our first beds were twins and when we moved to California we purchased a king sized bed and more chest of drawers. We built on this line as our needs for more bedroom pieces increased after our move from Mississippi to California.

Chapter 23

The Move to California

To get to California upon his Honorable discharge from the Army, JH drove the entire distance alone. The important fact here is the time that he made the trip. He left our apartment in Natchez, Mississippi, early Monday afternoon driving west to California. He called me on Wednesday morning just before noon, after driving the whole trip almost non-stop. I was petrified and immobilized that he took such a risk but relieved to hear of his safe arrival. His phone call, let me know was now at his Godmother's home in Oakland, California. He then went to sleep and called me when he awakened the next evening. He slept deeply to rejuvenate from the toil of the road and lack of sleep. His plan was to go out and look for employment the next morning. He wanted to get started in preparing for our move there while he stayed at his Godmother's home.

Getting settled

After a few weeks, he found work and called me to let me know so that I could call the moving company. My task was finish getting the household contents ready to be shipped to California. We planned to take all of our belongings in the moving van, except for what we needed for our immediate needs. Because I planned to fly, I only packed the Samsonite luggage set. It was still up to the task, even after college, teaching and now, moving. The travel plan was for me to fly with the baby girl, while I was in my fourth month of pregnancy. I was anxious, physically and emotionally ready to join him as soon as I could. We endured the first pregnancy with him stationed on base and wanted to be together through this one.

Pregnancy and the results

We were expecting our second child that summer of 1968. JH helped me pack all of the boxes we would ship before he left, to keep me from having the stress of that task. According to our plans I called the Mayflower Moving Company and had them move the entire household contents as soon as I got the word to leave. JH looked for an apartment, while he worked. Upon my arrival I helped in the search for an apartment. We were expecting our baby boy in July and I would be looking for a teaching job in Oakland for the start of the school year in September. We had our plans firmly in place and we were on our targeted timeframe. We found an apartment and JH worked while I put things in order, getting an obstetrician, making the appointments and getting ready for our new son. We were so happy, contented and expecting our son as we adjusted to our new goals of living life in Oakland, California.

Our fate was fatal. I went into labor at seven months in May on a Saturday just one day after seeing my doctor. I was told on the phone to meet the doctor at Doctors' Hospital in San Leandro, California where my doctor practiced. When I got to the hospital my blood pressure was sky high. They could not induce labor at the time because of all the symptoms. In the meantime, my young husband had to make a choice. The doctor asked him what he wanted to do, save the baby boy or save my life. To take the baby would have resulted in the baby living; to wait and work on getting me stabilized would put the baby in jeopardy. In the meantime my daughter was with JH at the hospital and he had to take care of her because we did not have another plan in place. We are saddened to say and to experience it again; as I share with you that we lost our son when I was just in the seventh month. It was traumatic for all of us, but more so to me. Our daughter was only two and a half years old and missed me, at the same time did not quite understand it all. My husband was devastated because he had to make that life choice decision. To top it all off I lost the ability to have more children. I lost my eyesight. I lost my baby boy and I had battle scars from something that I was not even aware of: Toxemia.

There were more traumas for our finances. My maternity insurance covered the entire pregnancy in Mississippi, because it was a group insurance. When I left Meridian, it became an individual policy and only covered the doctor's fees and not the hospitalization in California. I never used that nationally known insurance company ever again and will not recommend it to my enemies. My pregnancy complication was toxemic and with my blood pressure up, I could not deliver the baby. They had to wait until my pressure came down before they would proceed to operate. I had a cesarean. Our baby son did not survive! And I lost my eyesight because the pressure knocked my eye grounds out and for a time I only had peripheral vision. This insurance gave me the Blues because the individual plan had us in debt to the hospital for five thousand dollars. That was a lot of money and it was a whole lot of money in 1968.

My doctor knew the financial situation and had the hospital release me early. He carried me home to my apartment and helped me in where I had no help until my husband came home after picking up our daughter who stayed with a new found friend. The doctor true to his word came by our apartment the next week or so to check on me until I could get well enough to go to the medical office.

My young daughter and I had to learn to endure life without my sight until my eyes healed. Physical healing was over a two month period of time, emotional healing took much longer. My young husband worked, cooked, took care of all our needs, washed and folded clothes. He also did the weekly shopping. We were one mess, but blessed because, all of my situations could have been fatal. I am blessed to be alive. I thank God for blessing me with a supportive and caring husband. Ironically, my baby boy was delivered on my brother Pete's birthday May 19th. I survived!

We all have challenges in our life but God gives us the strength to carry on. I am thankful that I can acknowledge this fact. Even now as I share with you, this phase of my life causes me tears, as I write. As the story goes and also as life goes on, there are rewards of strength and perseverance. When I awoke from my operation and found myself not in the OB ward, but the surgery department, I was without sight. I could not see because the trauma of toxemia and high blood pressure knocked my eye grounds out. I really was devastated. My husband was at a great loss but he kept the faith and stayed the course. He knew what he had to do to survive and make a life for his young family. He had to make a decision few young men even have a nightmare about, let alone make as a life choice. JH worked two jobs for the remainder of the year. He did what he did and he had to move forward because that is what you did in order to survive.

Yet, I continued to be blessed in spite of these challenges. My goal was delayed and turned around but the game of life was not over. We still had a family. We still had our young daughter. My husband soon got a job at the post office to offset our ongoing unexpected expenses. I wrote my resume and submitted it to the Oakland School District. When I embarked on this task, I could not see very well but I had patience, determination and my husband's critiquing my writing and spelling. When I finished and got his approval of my resume, it was ready to be mailed.

A teaching position

A phone call and lots of prayers soon got me an interview with the superintendent at the administration office. I got the job in Oakland Unified School District at my choice school. The reason I said my choice is because the Superintendent gave me two choices. I was new to Oakland and new to the schools demographics. I chose the one in the flatlands rather than the one in the Skyline Area of Oakland Hills. I was content with this choice and it worked out well for me. One was predominantly black and the other predominantly white. It was not the race or color that helped me with my choice but the locality.

I really did not know my way around and the city of Oakland was very hilly and the streets on the north side were not easy to maneuver by car and certainly for me by bus. Our apartment was on 81st Avenue in East Oakland. Our daughter was to be enrolled in the Blue Bird Nursery eight blocks from our apartment and two blocks from the bus stop. Every day that we lived on 81st Ave., I walked carrying her in my arms to and foe. I took the transit bus to my school in Sobrante Park. September 1968, found me as a teacher of Physical Education for girls at Madison Junior High School in Oakland, CA.

Employment and earning a living

He soon got a better unionized job at Mack Trucks as a mechanic. By this time he needed to take a break from the stress that he endured for such a long time. In fact, his body told him that what he was doing was too much of a strain. In December of 1968 and before he went to work at Mack Trucking Company, JH had something to happen to his body that caused me to drive him to the emergency room at Kaiser Hospital. It was not clear what happened but he got a spinal tap and that was enough to let him know that he did not want to experience that procedure ever again. So we both worked like normal people and rested and enjoyed our employment, our family and our blessings that were ours.

In the summer of 1969 we were able to go back to Mississippi and Louisiana to visit our families. In October of that year, we moved into our new to us home in the foothills of Oakland. We brought a used car for me to cover the extra miles we had to go now that we were much farther from my school. I also found a nursery school that would transport our daughter to the kindergarten in our new school district when it was time for her to attend the school.

Financial and Educational Growth

We progressed financially and I educationally over the next years. I attended Hayward University, now known as the University of the East Bay, where I got my California Teaching Credential in 1970. While I was attending school for advanced credit to increase my take home pay, I also completed some other course work. By 1976, I had a Masters Degree in Physical Education. By 1981, I had an Adapted Physical Education Credential. At this time I changed careers from Physical Education Teacher to Adapted Physical Education (APE) Specialist. At the district level in Special Education, I worked with three other APE Specialist covering over one hundred schools both private and public. In 1985, I embarked on another credential. My goal was a PhD, but I settled for another Master's Degree. After reviewing the course, I was excited about the new Masters and subsequent educational growth.

Professional growth and leadership

The Educational Leadership Degree coursework at St. Mary's College of Moraga was inspirational. I was able to work on three administration projects and served an administration internship at an elementary school while in the program. From one of my projects, with the assistance of the APE Staff and our Special Education Manager I designed a Physical Education Handbook. This specific skills and strategies handbook was designed for inclusion of all students of Special Education in the regular Physical Education programs. We consulted, with Special Day Classroom Teachers. We collaborated with administrators, therapist and parents of students. We made determinations on whom and how much of needs a student was given in an Individual Educational Program (IEP). We also gave workshops and made a major presentation of our method of delivery of our services. We presented as a school district on our modality at the California State Conference of Health, Physical Education, Recreation and Dance (CAHPERD).

Our Department of all four Adapted Physical Education Specialist worked on this inspiring Handbook presentation. Our Handbook and supportive documentation for successful inclusion was received whole heartedly. The State Conference for the National Conference of Adapted Physical Education, presentation was in San Diego, CA in 1985. Every individual who attended were given one of our handbooks and those who did not receive one were sent one to their district. Our presentation changed the way many other school districts delivered Adapted Physical Education to their students. I did a second handbook for teachers in the Oakland School District, in conjunction with a project at an academy with friend and principal, Connie White. It was available for any school to incorporate into their school Physical Education program. The third handbook was a group effort with my friend and co-worker, Belinda Rector. We developed this at the district level and had input from Physical Education Teachers, Special Day Teachers and Pre-School Teachers. It was entitled, *Inclusion of All Students in Physical Education.* This title was developed for elementary and junior high school students.

According to the Tougaloo College motto, *we are Leaders.* My leadership in CAHPERD continued well into my retirement years. Every year since 1981 I was active in the Professional application of my field of employment. For many years I chaired many of the sections. My main focus was on Multi-Cultural which had to do with inclusion of all sections and all sports. Because of my Mississippi background of not being recognized and treated substandard, I was passionate that all participants in the organization were given credence. I was also a member of the national association for almost 50 years and am still a member. This is the professional organization for Health, Physical Education and Recreation (and Later) Dance, (AAHPERD) that I was introduced to as a student at Tougaloo Southern Christian College, which was the college name during those years. My work ongoing with active adults is directly related to the American Alliance for Health Physical Education, Recreation and Dance. For leadership, personal health and wellness, I continued to teach, mentor and promote, *Living Life Fit and Well.*

Part 11:
The Reasons to Return to Mississippi for Those Who Leave

Chapter 24

Returning Home to Mississippi

When JH worked for Mack Trucks, the entire working staff was given a two weeks winter break and we would go home during the holidays. We also went back to Mississippi and Louisiana for a two to four week vacation during the summer over the years. In those years JH's mother, Mama Inez looked for us to arrive in time for Christmas Eve. Her birthday was January 1st and this was special to her to see us during the holiday season. We did not disappoint her for as long as the perks lasted, at Mack Trucking Company. It was a wonderful time and dangerous living at the same time. For the 2,300 mile trip was often made in 35 to 40 hours when we were younger and took highway risks. However, this was one of the ways we maximized our trips on our returning home, back to Mississippi.

Employment changes

Sadly, Mack Trucks closed their facility in the early 1980's and we were asked to relocate to the state of Pennsylvania. I was not interested in relocating to the east coast. I enjoyed Philadelphia when I visited in 1961 for the National NAACP Convention but had no desire to live there. Eventually, Mack Trucks left the Bay Area which had great weather. Where Mack Trucks moved was an area that was cold and foreign to us. We were concerned for our well being because of the loss of great income and benefits but Mack was not our entire life. We had a home and friends and we were secure in my job in the Bay Area. Our choice was to remain in our home and make adjustments for our stability when Mack Truck Company closed. To move with the company could have made a big change in our living pattern and may have also allowed us to continue rather than stop our annual winter visits. We knew that this would happen to our trips back to Mississippi and Miss-Lou Area. However, we chose to be proactive during this challenging time. JH did not have a job, yet we made plans. Yes, we had audacity, desires and drive to make our lives a positive adventure. When I put it all in prospective, I know that it really was, faith. We had faith in God and would trust our future to his guidance, totally.

New Educational Quest

It was at this time that I enrolled in the University of Pacific to work on my Adapted Physical Education (APE) Credential that summer of 1981. Much to my amazement, I was successful in fulfilling all of the requirements for this credential because the majority of the coursework needed was completed when I received my masters in Physical Education four years prior. The time it took me to accomplish my goals for this coursework was just six weeks. I want to let you know that all coursework for the credential was accomplished in just those six weeks. This credential may have taken from one to two years for many other students. Because I was able to accomplish this goal so expediently, we had time to make other substantial plans for our lives.

It was at this same time that we took the opportunity to purchase property in the Lake Don Pedro Subdivision as an investment from the severance pay JH received from Mack. We could and would weather the transition until JH found another job. He got a severance and also qualified for funds for job training. In fact, it was a blessing to have the time to make life changes. During those Months he was off work he did not waste his time. JH went to school and learned how to construct, and build his own designs.

In the classes, he drew the genuine, real blueprints for our cabin. The blueprint drawing was a special skill that he was introduced to only during the class, yet he mastered it and produced the plans that passed the certifications to build our cabin. This project was a long term project that started while he continued the job training. He was able to start construction on the cabin with the help of neighbors and resulting lifetime friends. With their help we constructed the exterior. It reminded me of the time when my dad went to school after WWII and learned how as well as constructed our first home in Natchez, Mississippi on Ray Street.

I finished my coursework for the credential at the University of the Pacific (UOP), in Stockton and was identified as a student in the graduating class of '82. I finished my work during the summer session of '81 with all requirements met. I did not attend the ceremony for this certification. I was satisfied to have completed all of my course work and would be able to work as an Adapted Physical Education Specialist. Since we both had the remainder of the summer after my session was completed at UOP; we decided to go back home to Mississippi for a couple of weeks. We, along our teenage daughter were off on our trip for the summer once again, back to Mississippi!

Changes in circumstances

I wanted to change careers so I had to request a district transfer. This form had to be filled out before any teacher could make a change of schools. Before we left for our summer vacation to Mississippi, I put in a transfer for making a change at the central school district. My Goal was to change from Physical Education in junior high school to Special Education as an Adapted Physical Education Specialist (APE). Within just a week after our return from Mississippi, I was asked to be the teacher of Physical Education for another school, Roosevelt Junior High by the previous principal I worked with. I let him know that I would transfer to his new school. However, this was only with the understanding that I wanted to be relieved if a position became available in APE. My plan was to be relieved from the physical education position. My goal was to take the position as an Adapted Physical Education (APE) Specialist when I was accepted by the Special Education Department. He agreed, not having a clue that my next position would come so quickly. Neither did I know that it would happen so quickly. However, during the first week or so after I returned from UOP, I was so excited to share my new knowledge. My interest in this new position was so compelling that I called every day or so to connect with the manager of Special Education who directed the Adapted Physical Education Specialist. I remember his name because I contacted him so much. He also remembered my name as you will see very shortly. When I finished calling that Special Education Department everyone involved knew my name. I wanted to claim that job for myself and I was highly motivated to accomplish it. That is essentially why I made the request for the district transfer.

It was only the first six weeks of the school term in 1981 before I was called for the position and eventually became an APE Specialist. Ironically, this principal liked my program so well that he kept my name on his staff roll for the remainder of the year and hired only substitute teachers to carry out the guidelines that I set when I was the teacher of Physical Education. Well, I did not leave them totally because I was there for the remainder of the school year as the recreation specialist. My job was teaching and coaching gymnastics in the afternoon program in the gymnasium. I formed an allegiance with the male teacher of physical education at that time who also coached at various high schools. He was the first person that I recommended as a replacement when we lost our next Adapted Physical Education Specialist. He worked in that field and was a special friend for the remainder of his life. Ironically, his name was Hollis Green. Using the same initials was our ongoing joke. But it was a wonderful professional relationship!

Because of the new schedules JH and I had, we would not have the time for both of us to be off during the winter breaks as we had for so many years earlier.

Returning in 2006

However, we continued our trips back home to the Miss-Lou area in the summers from 1981 until 2006. It was that year, in 2006 that we visited home for the summer months and went back to Mississippi again in the fall of 2006. We went back to Tougaloo College at that time of the year to celebrate the 45th Anniversary of the Tougaloo Nine Sit-In. We had on that occasion a very special reason to go back to Mississippi. I shared with you earlier, that I had not had the opportunity to interact with my fellow schoolmates since the summer of 1961. For me the invitation was a very special time to go back home, to Tougaloo and interact with those who were a part of this historical event, the Jackson Library Sit-in of March 27th, 1961. The celebration was truly a momentous occasion that I looked forward to celebrating. I do not want to confuse you by giving you all of the specifics and details. However, I want to be clear on our many reasons to return back to Mississippi. One good reason I share information of the reunion with you is so that you may feel my emotions. Your ability to feel what I felt at that time is so important to me. I was blessed to be able to accomplish this feat that I longed for those many years. Here we were after all those years finally able to reconnect with the group of individuals who risked our lives together. We experienced challenges and hardships together. Now we could once again come back together with the blessings of Tougaloo College and the city of Jackson, Mississippi. JH and I were elated to finally be able to experience meeting the members of the Nine. We looked forward to the long awaited acknowledgment for our participation in the non-violent civil disobedience event of March 27th 1961. I have a special chapter to address this celebration and what it meant to me. I am trying to be personable with you yet it is so hard to open up and share all of the emotions that have been with me for 50 years. I want to clearly emphasis to you the importance of this Tougaloo Nine Event and results has had on me and my family.

We have had so many celebrations and deaths over the years, some for happiness and some for tears. None were as devastating as the reason for going back like this next one. My mom died before we left Mississippi so I cannot count that one in this documentation of back to Mississippi. Yet there were and still are many reasons for going back to Mississippi!

Death was always a reason

On May 27th, 2007, we had to make arrangements to return to Mississippi for the funeral of my dad, Rev. Over the years we traveled by personal vehicle, train and rental cars. Our choice of transportation varied according to the best need during those emotional times spent traveling back to Mississippi. We drove our personal Car, for the entire trip to Mississippi when we vacationed the summer of 2006. For our second trip in 2006, we took the Amtrak train to Houston, Texas and rented a car to Mississippi for the trip to Tougaloo College Tougaloo Nine 45th Anniversary. We also traveled in our motor home in 2007, on a vacation where we made planned stops at RV parks, various cousins' homes and even a week at a RV park in Las Vegas. We parked the RV in Fayette, Mississippi and rented a car to travel to Virginia to visit and witness the marriage of one of JH's brother on the memorable date of 07/07/07.

Now, this is something that I cannot explain and really did not want to bring up but the facts are there which is why it is such a mindboggling experience. Facts are just that, they tell but my emotions and memories of what are important. Be gentle with me if my facts and emotions cross over. The reality here is that I want to let you know about what happened to me and how I processed these actions. In 2007, when we drove our motor home back to Mississippi Dad was alive. I remember how excited he was to sit in the motor home and how much he enjoyed the experience of being in the vehicle. He suggested that we park the vehicle in his driveway while he went happily and excited along with us as we rented a car in Natchez. We then drove the car to Virginia for the wedding of JH's brother. When we returned, Rev drove with us to return the rental car.

It was in 2007, that we got the call to come home for my dad's funeral. For his home going, all ten of his children were in attendance. This was sad, happy and special, because we were all there together for the first time in some years. Although it was for my dad's home going, we were agreeable, cooperative and loving to his end of life. The toughest of the celebrations was my dad's home going. We went through this sobering but joyful home going of our Dad with the knowledge, that no matter our circumstances, we were all there!

My sister had plans to be married on my dad's birthday in December of 2007. As we know, my dad would not be there to give her away. JH and I took the train for this trip and rented a car in Houston, Texas. For Rachelle's wedding nine of us were in our sister's wedding party. I was Matron of Honor, and seven of our brothers walked her down the aisle. When the minister asked the question, "Who gives this bride away?" In a chorus, all brothers said, "We do". We were engaged in so much family celebrations in the year 2007. I had to call both JH's brother and DeEtter to get them to check each document to make certain that all of this happened in 2007. All of documents were dated in the year, 2007! The year was a tear jerker, as well as a time of great celebrations.

Travels and transportation

We came home to Texas, in January of 2008 for the funeral of JH's favorite nephew who died suddenly at a young age of heart problems. This trip was suddenly, so we just packed and drove down in our personal vehicle. This was not a regular visit so we returned home to California without visiting anyone back in Mississippi. On our next trip the summer of 2008 we rented a mini-van to Mississippi and back. We did not want to put the wear and tear on our personal vehicle and also had the opportunity to rent one that was more economical. Over the years, transportation was varied, and the trips were long ones but we used whatever means was best for the event we had to attend. Even when we went on the train, a rental car was necessary.

Reunions were a reason

For this trip, we had three reunions to attend. The details will be included later. The Beverly family reunion which is the family of Mama Tex, my dad's mother was held in Ferriday, Louisiana. The White family reunion which is the family of my granddad, Alfred White, my mother's dad was held in Vidalia and Natchez, Mississippi. The third affair which an event in itself, the Sadie V. Thompson School Era Reunion which was held in Natchez, Mississippi for all blacks who attended the school from 1954 to 1976, before schools were integrated. All three were in the month of July. We juggled our attendance and transportation schedule to make it to certain events of each reunion.

I share this with you because every trip was not a vacation. Some were joyous and some were emotionally filled. The main focus is that we made it back as often as we did and we thank God that over the years, we made all of the trips safely. Going back to Mississippi is more than just traveling there, it was roots. When you have a total of 15 siblings between us, aunts, cousins, nephews and nieces, returning home for various reasons became a necessity. As you can now see there were many reasons to return on our trips, back to Mississippi. We maximized our trips back home to Mississippi . . . just in case it was the last time. We were more than visitors: we were sojourners on a destiny . . ."Back to Mississippi"!

Part 12: The Tougaloo Nine

Chapter 25

The 45th Anniversary Celebration

The 45th Anniversary Program was the very first time that I knew anything about the group of the Nine, getting back together and being acknowledged since I left the college. The outline to support the yearlong celebration is in the Appendix. There, you will find the facts of the celebration, but I am sharing with you from my perspective. I wanted to share the information in this chapter to show you how a yearlong educational program was designed around the Civil Rights Movement started by the Tougaloo Nine. In a previous chapter of this manuscript I asked a question, where will we go from here? My answer to that question is what I plan to get you to think about. My perspective is in front of you. This is why I have written my feelings and life story around this question in, "Back to Mississippi". It was written to get you involved in the consequences as well as positive results for our actions with further answers to the questions, why the book and why now? First and foremost, I want to get your attention and to keep it.

I want you to continue to feel the emotions that were evoked by this very moving and historical series of experiences. The experiences were those started by the Tougaloo Nine in Mississippi but that was just the beginning. I am totally elated about the fact that this movement started so small in comparison to other non-violent civil disobedience events and was a very successful one. We salute those who followed with deadly results and had traumatic ensuing experiences such as the activities of the Freedom Riders and the ongoing Jackson movement. I knew of several students personally who were a part of the group that was physically hurt. When you live in a moment of reality, it stays with you. You want to aid those who were hurt but do not have the means or ability to do anything. So it was after so many years, that I could finally see that someone was looking and doing something to acknowledge what transpired by the actions of young students, just like me.

My commendations are given to the committee for the inclusive planning to highlight the educational format of the program designed in this 45th Anniversary. My sincere feelings were that it was a long time coming. Yet, I was happy that this acknowledgment finally happened. The recognition was a year long program of which one beautiful weekend was dedicated to the Tougaloo Nine Participants. When you read the appendix of the program, you will see that the year-long program was inclusive of many who made waves during the civil rights era after the Event of the Tougaloo Nine. To recognize so many was only fitting for all of this inclusion, because the Nine of us only started the movement. But, it took much more to get the results that finally happened.

For this acknowledgement, I was grateful. In fact I was honored to know that what we started sparked the beginning of educational platforms that can enlighten so many in positive lifetime appreciation. The Educational Project, "If you're Gon 'Be a Leader, Don't Stay Behind" _ Remembering the Jackson Civil Rights Movement was started in April of 2006. (Tougaloo College

2006)The schedule was inclusive of many who participated and was involved in the Total Jackson Movement which was started by the Sit-in at the Library by our group, known as the "Tougaloo Nine"!

In the fall of 2006, it was with delight and great anticipation for me when the invitation came to ask that I participate in the 45th Anniversary of *the sit-in that spurs the educational project*. For me this was something tangible, concrete and celebratory. After forty five long years of anticipation I finally got an invitation. After forty five years of wondering if anyone in Mississippi, let alone the United States of America or even the world remembered that nine black venerable teens and young adults stepped up to make a statement. Not just to make a statement but to move forward with all that we had to make a change, in Mississippi. We made a choice to put our lives on the line. We made a choice to die for the cause of civil rights that would benefit all. We were young, but we were savvy of the way Mississippians conducted the injustices towards all black citizens. My heart was heavy for the regret that I felt that no one had remembered before 2006. Sure, they may have made an acknowledgment on paper or somewhere, somehow in the brief look at the year 1961. But did anyone really acknowledge the life changing event in the light of the individuals of the Tougaloo Nine. Concerning the nine of us, I always wondered what had our lives been because of our choice for all of these years? Where were these Nine Students living and doing? What effect had this event had on their psyche? I only have my view and naturally I questioned what happened with the other eight. How did they cope? I had to put on a tougher physical self, because of what was bottled up inside of me. Now I ask the same questions for myself. First, did anyone remember the girl, named Geraldine Edwards who was determined to do her best as a student at Tougaloo College? Did anyone wonder why she did not attend the graduation during the '63 celebration and receive her diploma with her classmates? Did anyone even care? Why was there no follow-up to see how she fared after devoting time to make a change for all with the help of the fellow group of nine participants?

Did anyone even wonder where I was after all of these years? There is a well know commercial that pretty much says what I wanted to hear, did anyone care or listen when I spoke so clearly and determined with my actions on March 27, 1961? What about the Tougaloo Nine as a group or as an entity? Was there meaning for us after making such a dynamic change for the resulting growth overall for citizens of Mississippi?

The celebration was started as an, Educational Project for the March 27, 2006, 45th Anniversary of the Tougaloo Nine Library Sit-in. In order to learn more there is a need to be taught, introduced to or experience that knowledge. After all of the many years without a clue of how my actions made a difference for the other students, the college, the state and the south, I did not hesitate to commit to attend. My husband endured my reactions of disdain and neglect whenever, I saw the developments that were forged because of nine students who did not act out of selfish motives but because it was right. It was the right time to do so and it was right for the entire citizenry of the state of Mississippi. I wanted it to be clear that my long time mate and friend to whom I am married was also invited. We were one and from the very start he lived my emotions in delight for success, as well as the pain of not having anyone realize the contributions that I know were made with the blessings of God who sustained us.

To adequately support those emotions I experienced, there was much to be considered. During the ordeal there was the support of each other, the nine of us as we went through the situation. There was the support and guidance of our advisors, Medgar Evers and our Chaplain John Mangram. There was the college administration that did not dismiss us as students. There were the fellow students who endured our confinement in fear for all and perhaps their own destiny. There were our parents that endured our plight in each individual community. It was a very defining event and time. Yet, where was the acknowledgement from anyone because of what we endured to make that change? Over the years, I constantly, shared and enlightened my husband whenever, I got the opportunity regarding how my participation in the Tougaloo Nine Event affected me. I was especially traumatized when there were incidents that highlighted celebrations in Mississippi for the positive growth that has evolved since that time in 1961. I wanted to go because I finally would be able to say, *someone remembered.* So to the question, *is my husband, JH invited to take part in the celebration?* I was looking for a positive resounding answer of, *yes.* All of our married life, I had shared snippets and tidbits of this historical lifestyle changing event in the *Sovereignty State of Mississippi* with my husband!

I spoke often of how I wanted to see us, the nine reunited. It was amazing to me, that for the original photo we find everywhere acknowledging us as the Tougaloo Nine we were intertwined with a male, a female, and so on to include the nine of us in perfect togetherness. Have you looked at this image? We were situated physically as a cohesive group. We were compatible and in total integration as a body of participants. Simply put the Tougaloo Nine were a together group in all inferences. We were essentially one. Yet, over the years we were fragmented, not in attention to our belief in what we did or accomplished but in continuation of what we started. We all had to get through our college class work. We all had to make our way in the world we then found ourselves in. This was the world we dreamed would be better for us because of what we gave our time and physical self to accomplish. We now had a life and others now had the beginning of a better life. The college prospered as new students came and left with grand goals of making an impact on the world. Their world, the one we opened up for available jobs and living situations was the same one that we the nine did not have before we made our bold stand at the, *White-Only Library in Jackson Mississippi.*

It was only when we were contacted for this event that we were all with the exception of one able to communicate. It was with pleasure that I now could come back together with a group who basically made the same sacrifices, mentally and emotionally. It was then and only then that we could be a group again. We now had each other's contact information. We were nine young adults who made a choice to make a difference. Now that we were back together, we knew that our choice was a good one.

My actions were now acceptable to society because someone recognized that in some small way I needed this approval. Someone felt that what I did was worthy of making a celebration about. Imagine my delight to finally get some gesture of recognition. I felt appreciated. Do not get me wrong, I did not win a *Promotional Prize*. I simply was validated as an individual for what I participated in so many years ago. I was to be acknowledged for what I taught in the junior high school for so many years on being ethically right; yet did not know of any documentation that would let my thousands of students know my history for this thinking. I now had a platform or acknowledgment as a resource. Yes, I know what I did was creditable and beneficial. The yearlong celebration was documentation. I could now celebrate my participation in the history of Mississippi. Someone approved of what I contributed to, as the growth of justice for all who desired it. Many human beings have learned to thrive on just what was given to me with this recognition. Those gestures are approval, acknowledgment and appreciation. Appreciation is one of those gestures that this celebration gave to me. For this one generous gesture of giving I can say you heard my scream. You felt my pain not of self but of society interaction. You soothed my hurt, not of muscle and bones but acknowledgment. You let me know that you felt as I felt when you validated my actions for positive change in Mississippi. You gave me courage and fuel after all of these years. You acknowledged me as being normal in so many ways, I admit that I yearned for and needed. Now I push forward as I continue to fight for the injustice, the degradation, and also the acknowledgment of all who worked to stop those hurtful actions. There are still those who need support to be the best they can be, here and now. There are also those who require a positive pat on the back to stay encouraged. We know that basically, all individuals are the same because we all need the same nutrients. What this acknowledgment gave me was as vital as the air we breathe, the water we drink and the food we need to sustain life. I am rejuvenated by the show of love in the 45th Anniversary of the Library Celebration. For this acknowledgment I say, *Thank You* to all who planned this celebration. I needed and would have been okay without it; however there is always the need for lifting an individual up. There is always a need for a kind or encouraging word which says, to keep up the good work. I am quick to say, *do what you do because someone sees your contribution and are also encouraged.* I was validated bountifully by this celebration for what I did not get as a student in Natchez, Mississippi. I was not given any creditability over the years for my actions in Jackson. I can now be seen in the light of what my life has been, to give to others and give generously for ethical and civil rights posterity. But, I also stop here and say that in spite of my cry, scream or even pain for acknowledgment I am secure. For what the Tougaloo Nine accomplished, I have always been self-assured and determined to continue with my innate beliefs. My dad would have said I was, *strong willed* and my mom would say something like, *stubborn.* I say of myself, I am *determined and self-directed, thank you!* All through this manuscript you may have made a note of all the capitalizations inappropriately. They were not that I did not know better for standard writing. The point was to be emphatic and you could not hear my voice so I needed for you to read the tone of my words. I did relent and made as few as I could live with but there are still some. For me to share this is a part of who I am. *To your own self, be truthful*!

JH and I lived in the same geographical area most of our lives but did not know each other when the Tougaloo event occurred. He did not remember the event very well and I shared it with him as constant as newsworthy events were acknowledged! Now, I had the opportunity to have him be a participant in what I experienced as well as the ensuing results. He had not had the opportunity to visit the Tougaloo College Campus or even Jackson, Mississippi. On our many visits back to Mississippi, there were so many family members to see and the majority of them were in Louisiana and Texas. As a result, we did not venture east of Fayette, Mississippi where my dad, Rev and his younger family lived. Yet, each year that I returned to Mississippi, I always let my mind drift to the event of the Library Sit-in and the subsequent development in the area in which I visited. There was always a change to discover. I took notice of the positive changes and growth from year to year. Many may have taken the development of Mississippi for granted but for me, each new concept and acceptance was more than just some big step for me. Each new development socially, commercially, and residentially was feathers in my bonnet. A symbol of success where there was practically none when all this started in 1961.

When the anticipated itinerary was received from the Office of Institutional Advancement we were ready to follow up on our side of the planning. So we made our travel plans. This trip was made on the train to Houston, Texas. All through my sharing in this story, there has been no mention of flying. JH has a medical problem that lasts during and for weeks after a flight has concluded. This was not always true. We flew many times in years earlier to places and events. Our last airline trip was in 1995 to the funeral of JH's mother, Mrs. Inez. Since that time we stayed on the ground with wheels of many kinds. For the trip to the 45th Tougaloo Reunion, a rental car was secured in Houston. We drove from Houston to Tougaloo College in Mississippi. We made one stop, before getting there which was in Fayette Mississippi. Although my dad was not invited to this occasion, he wanted to know of any events where he could take a part. After checking the schedule, I knew that he could attend the panel discussions, which were to be held in the Woodworth Chapel. I let him know that the session I was scheduled to speak on was to be held on Saturday Morning between 9:00 and 11:00 a.m. He was just two months away from his eighty-eighth birthday and still drove himself around the Miss-Lou area.

My dad's intentions were to be in that audience for the celebration as well. He lived through the Historical Event of the Library Sit-In and he went through the emotional and physical constraints that were placed on all of our family. He lived in Mississippi and he would be the first to share that the intervention of the Tougaloo Nine started something that allowed the blacks and the whites to live harmoniously together. This is one man that took advantage of the opportunity to use the new found freedom of community and political involvement for the advancement of his communities. Not just Fayette, but also Natchez, Mississippi and Ferriday, Louisiana. In all of these towns he experienced firsthand what could be done by being involved and a participant in the community growth with expectations for all human beings to benefit. My dad could drive but my younger sister made the choice to come along with her two daughters and drive my dad to the college and back on that Saturday.

JH and I got to our destination, which was the Jackson Hilton Hotel. There were some interesting changes as we made our way north towards Tougaloo College. The new to me hotel was just about a mile from the campus. This was a real wake-up to my memory. When I was last at Tougaloo it was still in the county. After getting over the surprise of our surroundings we moved on. When we went to the front desk we were treated as dignitaries. No matter where and when I traveled, I always carried the attitude that my life was just as important as that of any other person. I have had to live with this attitude most of my life and it is not so strange to me after all of these years. However, much to my delight, this was the first time being back in Jackson, Mississippi for this kind of acknowledgement. Starting at that very moment I began to feel validated because of what I anticipated and received without hesitation. Once we arrived in the northern part of Jackson we went directly to the Hilton Hotel. I bring this up because there was so much commerce around the area that I had not envisioned let alone see it for myself. There was commerce of everything and everywhere. There were businesses that would sustain living on the outskirts of Jackson in nothing like what I left in 1962 as a student. It was such influx of commerce that it literally left me speechless. Here we were among growth and prosperity right outside of the gates of Tougaloo College. Now we were to be a part of this innovative setting.

We had been invited to this city from which I experienced being in a public facility as a jailbird in March 27th 1961 and now were to be honored. And honored we were to have my name, Geraldine Edwards Hollis already reserved and a room designated for me and my husband. We made the trip down and over to Jackson on our own arrangements. Remember, we did not fly which was the set-up that the college would have arranged for me alone. The hotel was inclusive of the both of us, one room and the two of us. The arrangements had been made by the college for the stay at the Hilton Hotel for this Historical Event. Here we were at a place and time that showed appreciation for who we were and what we did as students in 1961. I was in awe! Here we were in 2006 being acknowledged as Tougaloo Nine participants by the hotel clerk. Upon hearing my name, she went on to acknowledge me as a participant and shared her comments of gratitude. She was really a manager of the Hotel and for this position at this time in this place was one of the results of the actions made possible by the Tougaloo Nine and others in Jackson who continued with the struggle for equality. Her job was a direct result of those actions.

The atmosphere was humbling for both me and my husband as we received the Friday, October 13, 2006 edition of The Clarion Ledger from the hotel desk clerk. On the front page was a picture of the Tougaloo Nine group standing in front of the Jackson Library as a background while highlighting the incident. *The article stated the facts of what happened on March 27, 1961.* As you now know, *nine Tougaloo College students, dubbed the Tougaloo Nine, attempted to integrate the Jackson Municipal Library, sparking a civil rights movement in Jackson.* Reading this information made me feel proud and at the same time appreciated. Can you imagine, seeing myself in this positive light and being acknowledged for whom I was and what I did. We were delighted and could go to our room feeling like real celebrities. Afterwards we were graciously shown to our room and had the opportunity to rest from our journey. We had time to prepare for the celebration, a reception for Veterans of the Jackson Movement.

The celebration was held from 6:30-8:00 p.m. that night. It was at this special time, that we the Tougaloo Nine attendees would receive keys to the city. A grand Tougaloo Alumni Banquet was the event for that night. After not seeing my schoolmates for 44 years, I was really looking forward to seeing all of the Nine. However, before I arrived at the banquet I was still not sure how many of us would be in attendance. My curiosity was soon satisfied as I was able to meet and greet the seven out of the nine participants who were able to make it to this celebration. I personally was overjoyed to see each of my school mates. We met on the Banquet floor and greeted each other one to one. We came together again as a group with photos and acknowledgment of time and expressions that really were as stimulating as the mist from a gentle waterfall. It was refreshing and energizing at the same time.

The memories of what, who and when came together in mere moments. Here we were the seven of us who were physically able to make the trip, together in one room. The walls closed in for a moment as we who were among hundreds were in a sphere of togetherness, just the seven Tougaloo Nine participants. After forty five years we had the same spirit of a cohesive group the same as when we were students and facing our life changing challenges. We were there to celebrate and to be celebrated. Of all of us, surprisingly we had no problems at all recognizing each other. Thankfully we all just seemed to have drifted in a suspension of time as far as weathering the age game. What a blessing to be able to say that we all could walk and with full gait. Our smiles were complete with a white flash of natural looking teeth. Some of us had sparkles in our hair and our girth was not out of proportion.

Life served us all well in that category. I relished the time we were given to reunite and at such a prestigious occasion.

Surprisingly to all of us, we were showered with attention, two ribbons, and not one key but two keys to the city of Jackson, Mississippi. One key and a Proclamation were from the City of Jackson and the other was from the Jackson City Council. This is the same city that arrested us, jailed us, and had court to determine our fate. Our participation and subsequent results caused us to be snubbed or shut out both socially and economic in some of our communities. Some of the nine were not able to continue with their course work. There were various reasons for which I am not truly knowledgeable. Evelyn had her reasons and James had his reasons. For me, my three year and three summers plan was continued. However, I refused to send home for more money the first week of the third summer and was surprised that I did not fall out for mal-nutrition. But I did not let my parents know this. It was a blessing that I was able to finish my education and to even find a job because money was really tight for my parents at that time.

Despite the consequences of our participation in the White Only Library in March 27, 1961, I was finally hired at a school in Meridian, Mississippi for the 1963 school year. I began to work during that year, despite the situations of continued civil rights demonstrations that were happening. Now, all of this dialog was a reflection to let you know that the Civil Rights Event was and did make demands on our families for various reasons.

Although we had a wonderful reunion we were saddened because there were only seven of us in attendance. One member of our group, Evelyn Pierce Omar was contacted at her home in Michigan, where she was ill but was a participant on the phone and commented on her past involvement at the Saturday panel discussions. Joseph Jackson was not able to be found at that time. We were prayerful for his life and missed him but with hope that by the next time we chanced to meet he would also be a part of the group.

This very profound occasion allowed us all to express what we were and had been feeling. With deep regret for the years passed, we agreed to keep in contact. I personally have all of the other seven as e-mail contacts and some as social network friends. This event left us with a rewarding feeling; we had gratification for the change which was a long time in coming. Can you imagine our emotions after not seeing each other for 45 years and to come to an occasion that was such a contrast from the original event? At the Hilton Hotel room and convention center we were surrounded in splendor in a facility that would not have allowed us to come in for a celebration and to be honored for what we were previously, jailed for. This was truly, a great change, for the members of the Tougaloo Nine, the city of Jackson and for the State of Mississippi. I was delighted and my schoolmates showed the same degree of satisfaction.

JH was not the only spouse there for this historical celebration. Albert bought his family which included his wife, a son and a daughter along. Meredith brought along his wife. We all had times that we could gather and reflect on ourselves, our families, our careers and our joy of coming together again in a celebration such as the 45th Anniversary there in Jackson, Mississippi.

The occasion was happy, festive and celebratory and at the same time sober and sad that we had to wait 45 years to be recognized for what led to the social and economic growth of so many Mississippians. Many young citizens never knew how *Black Citizens* were treated in 1961. For the seven of us to be there in that place and time was a testament that the Sovereignty State of Mississippi made the 180 degree turn for all humanity.

It was far better to be acknowledged than it was to be ignored. It was better to learn the history of a life changing event that clearly benefited the blacks as well as the white citizens. Gratefully, Leslie B. McLemore, a Jackson city councilman and director of the Fannie Lou Hamer National Institute on Citizenship and Democracy at Jackson State University, was appreciated when he stated that the recognition was long overdue. I welled up in tears at being able to hear those words from Mr. McLemore. Here again, I heard that what I did along with my school mates was validated as worthwhile as I already knew that it was. The Fannie Lou Hamer National Institute in Jackson has been doing what it does for citizenship and democracy but it is one thing to read about recognition. It was a wonderful feeling of validation to be truly recognized with celebration. The institute was also an event co-sponsor.

We were given the best of acknowledgments by the Tougaloo Alumni Association, The City of Jackson Mississippi and the City Council. All of us the seven representatives present for the 45th Anniversary of the Jackson Library were appreciative of the City of Jackson, Mississippi. Both Evelyn Pierce Omar and Joseph Jackson were not in attendance! The seven of us who attended had a high degree of sincere gratitude for the long awaited acknowledgement. For this, I personally am Thankful. I know that the members of our Tougaloo Nine Group share my sentiments. Thanks again to the City of Jackson and city council members for taking the time to let us know that we really were appreciated for the risks we took to make a difference in the lives of blacks, whites, and everyone in the state of Mississippi!

On this occasion, I saw and met with my co–participants for the first time as I remembered, since the sit-in all together with those in attendance since the March 27th Event while in Jackson, Mississippi. Forty-Five years is a long time to remember all of the details and not have written documentation. This is a work of memory and documentation of facts from the news media and talking over the years with my husband. Fundamentally, Back to Mississippi, is my recollection of my emotions and how the event affected me personally.

Others may view the experience from their own perspective. I am thankful for all the experiences. I know that my participation made a difference in the life of many in the nation, the state of Mississippi, the city of Jackson, and Tougaloo College.

The Tougaloo Nine attendees for the weekend celebration were scheduled to speak in the Woodworth Chapel on the Saturday panel discussions. I was in the session, Panel One from 9:00 am until 11:00 am along with Moderator: Rev. Ed King, James *Sam* Bradford, Albert Lassiter, and Evelyn Pierce Omar who participated via Phone.

It was gratifying for me to learn that the history of the participation of the Tougaloo Nine was being presented in this educational format. It was so great that Sam, as we call James Bradford, who lives in Jackson Mississippi, was able to bring some authenticity from our point of view over the years and especially for the year long program. Not because Sam was the only one who could but the one who was accessible of the Tougaloo Nine participants. The remainders of the Tougaloo Nine Participants were spread out over the various states, which was a great inconvenience to say the least to be a part of this year long program. Acknowledgment of participation in educational venues comes with financial support from one source or another.

It has been my experience that when it comes to financial support for education there was and still is a deficit. Having retired from the physical educational arena I cannot begin to compare the resulting prized students who make it big financially for their sports skills. Those skills were first learned in a Physical Education setting in the playing fields and on the courts of communities' schools. I am convinced that my justification supports why the Educational Programs are not supported as other facets of living and commerce in our United States. Basic education, like the pre-civil rights of so many citizens was not appreciated as the important phase of life that it really is.

My dad, Rev. Simmel Edwards along with my younger sister, Rachelle and my two nieces, Ramonnesha and Makyla were in attendance of the panel on that Saturday morning. When all the morning panelists finished, my dad stood and gave an expression. He was a proud dad and wanted everyone to know that, Geraldine Edwards Hollis was his daughter. He complimented the Office of Institutional Advancement for the Educational Forum and recognition of what the Tougaloo Nine did for the advancement of civil rights for all in Mississippi. I guess that I am a little like my dad. No one else to my memory stood to have a word from the floor but my dad saw his chance and seized the moment. He was always on target and right on time to address an occasion. It would be his first and last time making a statement at Woodworth Chapel at Tougaloo College in Tougaloo, Mississippi. *Rev, Simmel Edwards died on May 27, 2007, but he had no regrets! He was the proud dad of all ten of his children!*

We had some very soul searching and provocative statements to make that Saturday morning on the panel discussions. To my delight in this digital age with research of the event, anyone could get the media perspective of what was said at that educational discussion. My schoolmates acknowledged that I did as usual, talk for quite a while and that what I had to say brought in some humor. On the day of the incarceration, we had to have some humor. I was quoted by my classmates and the media that I made a big attempt to have humor. All of us as participants got another laugh as we revisited the situation. We were in a situation when we were jailed that we did not know the results of our actions. We each acknowledged our feelings about the event of incarceration as we expressed the theme for the morning program.

Our day was flowing but we had a compact schedule. After the morning panel discussion, which included the talk by my dad we went off to lunch. I said goodbye to my dad and family as they only stayed for that session. The Third Annual Kincheloe Luncheon Symposium was at 11:30 am and our group the Tougaloo Nine was recognized there also. When I was a student at Tougaloo, the Kincheloe Building was just a small building with plans for a larger facility; it was so gratifying to see the completed Science Building. We were in the company of scientist of great contribution to society yet they took the time to give us a small part of their program. This was very gratifying to me for this additional acknowledgment and the food was excellent. Speaking of food, the day of additional activities were like dainty savory tidbits of a high tea. It was elegant and satisfactory because all of this just heightened my appreciation. We did not have to worry about the timeline because our schedule included the facilitation of all of us being driven around the campus in order to be fresh for each event. I loved the sidewalks which were now more than when I attended back in the 1960's. There were more buildings and updates to some of the older ones. JH and I chose to walk to the next panel discussion back in Woodworth Chapel after leaving the Kincheloe Luncheon Symposium.

The Panel Two discussion was from 1:00 pm until 4:30 pm back in the Woodworth Chapel. The afternoon Session was Moderated by Professor Richard *Dick* Johnson. Schoolmates participation in this session were; Ethel Sawyer Adolphe, Meredith Anding, Jr. Janice Jackson Vails and Alfred Cook. This time I got to sit back and listen to all of them. It was great to listen to each and see the remembrances of our Library Sit-in. It was even better to hear of the educational leadership guidance and contribution each one made in their careers. We all summarized that our contribution to the resulting change in the state of Mississippi made a tremendous difference. We all went to various parts of the United States; however, the participation was always in our minds and hearts that we were instrumental in making a difference in humankind on that day and in our lives. It was great to see the families of those who also came along. JH was not the only spouse that wanted to experience this momentous event of celebration!

The culmination of the Tougaloo Nine 45th Anniversary was the Sunday 9:30 a.m. Woodworth Chapel for Founders Convocation. It was a special treat to hear the outstanding group sing the traditional Hymns and Gospel songs that were always an inspiration when I attended Tougaloo College decades ago. Afterwards we looked over the campus and noted the many positive changes that had also been made. JH and I were then treated with the other Tougaloo participants, family, faculty and staff at the President's House. It was a very fitting finale to our awesome celebration. The President, Dr. Beverly Wade Hogan an alumna, was the first female President of the prestigious college. Tougaloo College was known nationally as, *The Cradle of the Civil Rights Movement in Mississippi!* We had a time after the dinner to again reflect and interact with each other. Before leaving Tougaloo while at the president's home there on campus, I presented President Hogan with my personal collection of documents from the *Jackson Library Sit-In* and media prints. My donation was for the collection to be placed in the, Mississippi Civil Rights Museum, which was to be located on the Tougaloo College campus.

For me to give up all of those original documents which consisted of magazines and newspapers had to be a great sacrifice. Not only did I carry the emotions of the event in my memory and heart but I carried those originals from Mississippi to California and kept them in pristine condition because they meant a great deal to me. They were my legacy, now that I have put my memories and feelings down, I feel vindicated and secure in the knowledge that my personal bit of history is secure in infinity. What do you think?

To address the 45th year Theme: *If you're Gon' be a Leader, Don't Stay Behind-Remembering the Jackson Civil Rights Movement,* I was so elated. I was validated and proud to be a part of this acknowledgment. I am determined that this, Jackson Library Sit-In, was evident of my desires to be a leader in making a difference as a way of life. Over the years, I have not been able to live life in contentment. At every opportunity, I have advanced in Education and delivery of the education modality of which I prepared myself for. I truly am grateful for being naturally prepared to assist others in finding their best self by being prepared to be a, Teacher of Life Skills, no matter the subject. *You can't lead, where you can't go*! Tougaloo, College was for me the way to go!

I have always kept Tougaloo in my heart. No matter what institution of higher learning that I attended, Tougaloo was the foundation to the quest for making a change not only for me but for the lives that I had the opportunity to reach. It was only when we got back together in Jackson at the 45th reunion that I was reassured that the Tougaloo Nine participants were all true leaders in their chosen fields. I had no idea of what their lives had turned out to be. It was great to see all of the seven who was in attendance and to hear from the one who participated in a phone call during our presentation. I learned that we all had our challenges and our successes. We all felt a strong bond for our participation in the Library Sit-in and to our Alumni. This is what I carried away from the 45th Anniversary Celebration. March 27, 2011 was

50 years and another milestone to celebrate the efforts of nine students from Tougaloo College and the subsequent movement that ensured. Tougaloo College continues to be known nationally as "The Cradle of the Civil Rights Movement in Mississippi"! This is my remembrances of the 45th Anniversary Program in honor of the event made by the Tougaloo Nine students from Tougaloo College of Tougaloo, Mississippi, March 27, 1961.

There is an appendix of the schedule of programs and workshops which were a noble attempt to bridge the gap of participation and celebration of the proponents of Civil Rights in Mississippi.

This Educational Project, *If you're Gon'Be a Leader, Don't Stay Behind _ Remembering the Jackson Civil Rights Movement*, was started in April of 2006. The schedule was inclusive of many who participated and was involved in the Total Jackson Movement which was started by the Sit-in at the Library by our group, Known as the, Tougaloo Nine!

The conclusion of the year long Education Project concluded on Thursday, November 2, 2006 at Jackson State University with Panel Discussions: *Where do we go from here*? To answer this question as a fact and also from my perspective this is my answer:

Tougaloo College is and always was a very special school. Tougaloo was founded in 1869. A private, historically black, coeducational four year liberal arts institution, located in Madison County on the northern edge of Jackson Mississippi.

It is reported and documented that, more than 66% of Tougaloo graduates enter graduate or professional school immediately after earning their under graduate degrees and 100% of students pass the PRAXIS teacher education examination. As you remember, I had no problem securing my Mississippi Teaching Credential. Tougaloo College is one of the top five producers of female graduates with degrees in physics and one of the top twenty institutions in the nation whose graduates earn their PhDs in the Sciences. For those who only know what you have been able to learn from me from reading, Back to Mississippi, Tougaloo College instills this characteristic of striving for excellence. Tougaloo has produced more PhDs through the Mellon Fellowship Program than any other Historical Black Colleges and University. Tougaloo is a leading producer of professionals working in the state of Mississippi, including over one-third of health care professionals, attorneys, educators, and leaders of civil and philanthropic organizations.

Among Tougaloo College eminent Alumni are the Tougaloo Nine and yours truly, Geraldine Edwards Hollis. I retired from Oakland, CA Unified School District, with Administrative Leadership in Adapted Physical Education at the district level, consultant, workshop and projects leader, co-author of handbooks for teachers of both Special Education and regular students in Physical Activities. In retirement, my contributions are those of community leader, Director of Fitness for Active Adults and Sharper Brains Program, model of living life fit and well through healthy living, as well as a lifelong volunteer for programs to enlighten humanity. My life work has been to give, reach and teach; to enlighten and to stay ahead of the learning curve. My experiences as a member of the Tougaloo Nine was a foundation builder for where I found myself as a new teacher, administrator and now as an author. My goal has been implemented by default because I always found it better to lean forward than to stumble backwards. To address the question, *where do we go from here?* My Answer: *Forward!!!*

Fifty years and we still have more to do in our society to address the rights of all citizens to have the respect and due justice that is a constitutional mandate. Why this book? Because I want to let you know what you may have assumed but can now read from someone you know who personally went that way. Why now? Because, time is short and the need is still there now! After reading my ideas and sharing in my actions did you hear me loud enough to keep sharing this concept as a way of life? Did you feel my pain of not having the tools to reach the heights I desired because of degradation, suppression and second class citizenship; yet with determination, mentoring and guidance went to the uppermost acknowledgement just because someone cared? It is my goal to spread seeds of, *can do* to you. You can help be a part of the solution to move humanity forward!

Part 13: Back to Mississippi Journey or Destiny

Chapter 26

Making a trip not easily forgotten!

We have made so many trips to Mississippi over the years starting with the summer of 1969. I always liked the term, going home. JH and I have been away from both our families since the early sixties. We looked forward to going back to Texas, Louisiana, and Mississippi every year and when we were able to, we would go twice a year. We came in the summer and brought our daughter, Thelma. We came in the winter for ten years when JH worked at Mack Trucks. His work schedule allowed us the two weeks off to go that was at the time of the school winter vacation. During those trips we always left on the eve of the twenty second of December, which was JH's Birthday. We arrived on Christmas Eve at his mother's house, in Ferriday Louisiana. We very seldom let her know that we were coming. She expected that we might come and was always prepared. She had our favorite meals ready when we arrived. One meal in particular was Turnip Greens, cornbread, creamed corn and fried catfish. You could bank on that.

JH's mother, Inez had eight children. JH is the oldest. She treated them all special. They all had her special touches of their favorite foods. She was a very special mom. To me she was not a mother-in-law, she was a mother. This was very precious to me because my mother passed in 1963. I met JH and his family embraced me and also my entire family. Despite the fact that there were eight children she always welcomed more. Would you believe that my dad and JH's mom knew each before she married Mr. Hollis? When I or both of us were not around, my dad and brothers always made a stop at the Hollis home in Ferriday. There was a blending of families which made our bond even stronger. Our daughter Thelma was her first grandchild. Thelma was the first baby in the Hollis household and as a result she was surrounded by family and lots of love. Mama Inez was such a loving grandmother also. She loved Thelma as much as a grandmother could. Mama Inez passed at the age of 80 in 1995. That was a summer that we made the trip two times. Her memory is embedded in the life that I enjoy today. JH is a part of her in soul and spirit. My dad was always around the Hollis household whenever he visited Ferriday. Especially after Mama Inez died, he continued to look in on the younger Hollis adults. There were three sons still living in several of the houses that were properties of Mama Inez. Rev would keep an eye on them and let JH know how things were going from time to time. We were all a very close family and Mama Inez was a very important part of us!

Ferriday was our first stop during those years when Mama Inez was alive and we traveled south. We always spent our time in Natchez with my dad, his wife and family. My dad and his family moved to Fayette, Mississippi and I continued to make my stays at the house in Natchez. It was our home address from childhood. "Ray Street was our first and only home in Mississippi, it was something else." My brother John and his wife Vergie brought the house from my dad and his wife DeEtter. John continued to host all the Edwards and many other relatives on their visits home to the area from all over the nation. The home at Ray Street was the place where we all met and continues to be a place of welcome for all of us when we all come together, back in Mississippi. The house in Fayette was a place to visit; but the very familiarity of the Ray Street address made you feel the warmth and security of home in Natchez, Mississippi!

By now if you have been keeping up with my continued emotional dialog, I now want you to focus with me on our visits back to Mississippi in 2007. There were so many I could not keep count. I really, had to call several relatives to document the deaths, weddings and anything else that had a certificate.

However, on May 27th, 2007 we received a real shocker. My sister Rachelle, who is the youngest of my dad's children called me. I knew that the reason must have been very serious. Not just by the tone of her voice but also by the fact that we did not communicate by phone calls. There is an age gap between my sister and me of 33 years. She is my dad's baby but her mother and I started having children the same year. She is more like a niece to me rather than a sister. Her children are much closer and we talk quite a lot of the times when I call because when they are at Rev and DeEtter's they usually answer the phone. My sister Rachelle and I do not have those sisterly conversations, but neither do any of the younger brothers. My conversations are usually about and of their lives with their mom who is my friend.

DeEtter was my Matron of honor at my wedding. She has always been a friend and I have never acknowledged her as a step-mother but only as a friend. My sister Rachelle and I exchanged messages from her mother or her daughters for the majority of our conversations. I talked with my nieces and my sister got the messages from them or her mother. The majority of my interactions with my younger siblings are more on the same level as nephews and with Rachelle as a niece.

Rachel's call to me was to tell me something I was not ready to hear. What she gave me was the heartbreaking news that our dad had passed. I have experienced death in the family and even friends many times before but this time I was numb. My feeling of numbness was the result of my disappointment. I was hurt and disappointed not that my dad died but that I could have been with him for some of those precious days before he died. After learning that he was home from the Veterans hospital we knew that we needed to come home earlier than the usual time. We always came after my granddaughter's birthday June 28th and before July 4th. So, my plans were to come back to Mississippi around the middle of June. I made plans to come home in time for Fathers' Day to have time with my dad which would have been about three weeks away. During almost the entire year of 2007 up to the time of the phone call, we were aware of my dad's condition and knew that we would spend a longer time with him that year than normal. On one of our many conversations, I had talked to my dad in-depth and let him know of our plans for Fathers' Day. Both JH and I felt certain that he was doing well enough to keep our plans to come at that time.

Now, I was so disappointed with myself, that I had waited too late to come. I regret literally, that I delayed my plan to come back to Mississippi! Of all the years, we had come back home, this year was no different. I had no responsibilities to keep me from coming, the time, finances or even the transportation would not have been an issue. We just made plans to come down to make our usual rounds when more family came down for the Fourth of July. Since there were so many family members to see when we came down we tried hard to schedule our visits when we could see the largest number of cousins who also came back for vacation and this was primarily before, around and after the Fourth of July. There was no reason that I could not have come home to Mississippi to see my dad if only I had known that his time would be so limited. As you may remember, I lovingly called him by his title, Rev for as long as I can remember. I began to do this because he was our pastor and naturally, everyone called him Reverend so I just shortened it and said Rev as his name at home, at church and all of my mother's children referred to him as Rev. Now I want to take you back with me to this loss, which was so profound to me.

The date was at the end of January 2007, that Rev was rushed to the Jefferson County hospital in Fayette, Mississippi. This is where he lived with his wife, my friend and the mother of my three youngest brothers and my only sister. Rachelle is the youngest of the 10 living siblings fathered by my dad between Dee, his wife and my deceased mother, Thelma. Oh yes, my daughter was named after my mom, Thelma. So, before the call from Rachelle, we went through the times of hospitalization and keeping in constant contact with my dad.

Yes, I was numb because Rev was looking forward to our coming down for his time with us. He was possessive of his special time with me on the phone or even every time we visited back in Mississippi. We came home at least once a year and some years more. It just depended on the family special occasions or death in the family. Finally, when Rev became hospitalized and was moved to several facilities, we changed our plans to come before Father's Day to spend more time with him. We made our final, so we thought plans when he came home and was seemingly doing better.

When we first learned of my dad hospitalization he sent word for me and my brother to come home. He was first diagnosed with what was believed to be a stroke. But I talked to him long distance while he was in the hospital. We always talked long distance every week and sometimes more. I walked in the mornings for my aerobics about five days a week. With the two hour difference, my call at 6:00 a.m. Pacific Time was perfect for Rev. He would become impatient if Dee answered the phone and talked to me for too long of *his* time. He was not willing to share our telephone calls, because he knew that it was our special time together.

Rev was taken to Jefferson County Hospital which was a regional Hospital in Jefferson County in Fayette where they lived. He then was moved to the Regional Hospital in Natchez, Mississippi which was better equipped, that very night. He was later transferred to the Veterans Hospital in Jackson Mississippi. This all happened in just a couple of days time. The Veterans was his Hospital of choice for all of his medical needs. My dad often went to the VA Hospital just to get an overall check-up. Being allowed to stay from three days up to a week, he would jokingly say it was his way of getting a vacation. It was in many ways true, because when he was there he was able to relax and interact with Veterans who were also in World War II. It was while he was at the Veterans Hospital, that we talked in depth on many soul searching subjects. He shared so much with me during the talks we had. I called more while he was there at the Veterans Hospital. However, the time was not always in the morning as was our usual schedule. He would sleep more while he was at the VA and I did not want them to awaken him. He always stated that I was to call and have them wake him because as he said often, He could go back to sleep. My dad was really that kind of dad, even to the end.

I did not have inkling that the end was so close and this is what was so upsetting to me afterwards. He was truly a remarkable physical and humorous individual. He loved talking to people, and so do I. He had no hesitation in talking in public, and neither do I. My dad always set his own standards in clothing and head gear and so do I. My dad was a very supportive dad for all of us and for the younger set he was more generous than with the oldest children. Money and financial support was the difference. Our Mom did not work and Dee was a Teacher. We all had challenges but dad was a 100% supportive father to each in individual ways. For me and the older sons, we had a dad that was the best athletic supporter of any parents that I knew. Above all he was always in all of our lives every step of the way. He supported us and we all tried to be just as supportive to him. It was nothing for me to send whatever he wished for, he knew this and he had no problems asking. He walked around the town of Fayette for long periods of time. When he would wear out a pair of walking shoes he would just let me know to send him a pair. I knew the size and best brands and I would not hesitate to send them to him.

For me to not come to see my dad was so hurtful and took me to a level, I wish that I had not taken. During the times that my dad was able to come to California, I sent for him about every two years for a visit. When he came I also sent a ticket for someone to accompany him. My dad was a very special dad and he let everyone know of our close relationship. He really knew that he was special to me. JH would buy him a suit almost every year and he loved being dressed in his fashionable attire at all times. Fathers' Day was always a special time in our family and he looked forward to his celebration with great anticipation. We were not usually there at that time but he always looked for his special presents in the mail. This man went to the Post Office himself because he loved getting his jewels of special goodies out of the box himself. He often reminded me of how I felt to get the boxes from home when I was a student at Tougaloo. He was not hard to please. He just was delighted to be appreciated as he was by me and JH.

When my dad was younger, he would also spray himself with cologne because he enjoyed smelling good as he called it. *He was a joker*, as I shared how he met my mom on the Mississippi River Bridge and bet his friend that he could get to talk to my mom. As you remember his joke became a reality for which I am thankful. As a result, I was his first bundle of joy. How could I miss the opportunity to go and see him while we could still talk and hug and look into his eyes with the ring around the iris? At the Veterans Hospital, they determined that he did not have a stroke but was diagnosed as having a cyst on his brain. We let my dad know that we would come home and spend more time with him when we did come. Because it was a growth, it caused him to experience phenomenal brain changes. He could take me back to his life experiences down to the clothes he wore or the food he ate and at the same time tell me how it looked and smelled. During his stay in the hospital we talked on the phone as we usually did long distance each time for as long as he could stay awake. During those talks he would share those precise details he remembered in minute details. These were the things that happened to him as a child over eighty years before. I enjoyed his stories of his life as he remembered being a boy and of things I did not know about myself when I was around two or three. I relished those times he was able to converse, communicate and talk on the phone when he was not asleep or in therapy. He stayed at the Veterans Hospital for over a month. He was sent home and we felt that he was doing better, but it was not to be so.

While at home in Fayette, Mississippi, he had the care of all of his younger sons and daughter to support his wife. Rachelle was a certified Nurse and was continuing her education. It was a good setting for Rev's condition and he was surrounded by love and care. All of my brothers were able to visit him except for the one who lives in California very close to me. Those remaining ones who were in the south all live in the state of Mississippi and one in the Miss-Lou area. They all lived within one to three hours away. My brother out here in California and I, were the only ones not there during the time we considered his convalescence time.

When I got the call from my sister I had tickets for the train trip and return already in the system. I had only to pick up the tickets. The only thing we had to do was to change the tickets to the next departure time. As you can imagine, I was devastated. I called on my dear niece who made the changes we needed. Our change in plans was made with the same itinerary. We were able to get a train on May 29th and traveled for a day to Los Angeles where we spent the night near the train station, at the Plaza Hotel. Our trip took us on the train to Houston, Texas. We boarded the train in Los Angeles to Houston, Texas. Inez, our niece went online and secured our rental car in the downtown Houston area not far from the train station. JH's nephew, Roosevelt Jr., picked us up at the train station and took us to the rental car site where we departed for Mississippi.

We were coming home to Mississippi not to meet and greet my dad as we first planned, but to celebrate his home going. Over the years from 1963 I celebrated the Home going of my mother, Thelma; my adopted mother, Hattie; JH's dad Alonzo; JH's stepdad, Mr. E.B. Thomas; JH's mother Inez; my adopted dad, John and finally my dad Rev. The bottom line is that we are all destined to going home! We are not here to stay!

Life is a journey with the final destination set in place. It is not the trip but how you make the journey. We all travel along the lifespan of time. Our choices and decisions are what determines how the journey progresses. On May 29, 2007 my journal read: *Good-bye Daddy, be at peace. You wanted to go. God granted your wish to go home at 9:00 p.m. May 27, 2007. We know you loved us. We all knew that we were loved. You showed it in all you did and how you nurtured us as we grew. Being your first allowed me to know that we were a challenge. You met the challenge and you gave us the guidance to successfully make our way.*

Again, I must say that although we have a flaw in our plans we must continue to go forward. What I got from this experience was what I share continually, live in the presence, remember the past but continue to plan for your future. For my dad, it was not the end; he always had plans of a reunion of another kind.

Chapter 27

The Reunions

The irony of the back to Mississippi sign we read as we crossed the state line from Louisiana was *bold* and confidently stated, *It's like coming home!* Coming home to Mississippi, Louisiana and Texas was a part of our lives. We made this trip yearly, every year and with thanksgivings because it was a blessing to do so. The trip was something that we did every year and sometimes twice depending on what was going in our life or our families. You can conclude that we really looked forward to and enjoyed our trips back to Mississippi.

This year was the same, yet it was different. This year made a difference in my life. Our agenda was broadened by the combining of multi-family events. There was the beginning of three reunions that were planned just for the summer of 2008. When we look back we truly had a wonderful time, meeting and greeting family members and friends. The reunions were all in the month of July. This month was always a special time for me, as I relished the summer for the freedom, connection to fun, play and interactions. Summers were special even in college. Reunions were just as special and so were the family and friends we were able to connect with.

The reunions were the Beverly Family, the White Family and the impressive Sadie V. Thompson High School Era Reunion. The SVT High School was especially for the blacks to attend in the now integrated Mississippi town of Natchez. The SVT Reunion was the blacks' method to connect and keep in touch for those who lived in that era. For both the, Beverly and White reunions, we met family that we had no inkling we were related to. Some grew up in the same locality and we were unaware that that we were related. We also left with photos that were taken and collected. Enough to last a long time in our memories as well as our photo albums. We made a marathon of visits while we were in Mississippi, Louisiana and eventually, Texas as we worked our way westward from our trip back to Mississippi.

To all of our family members who asked us when were we coming back home, we just smiled. The previous ones that we made in 2007 were just about to put us in the mindset to go somewhere else for our next summer trip in 2009. We knew that we now needed a real vacation. We love all of our family members but we felt overwhelmed by that time of remembering the signage, *it's like coming home,* which was profound because of all that we had experienced the last two years. We had the journey and the experiences. Not to be mean or arrogant but what we needed next was not more of coming back to Mississippi! *We needed a vacation!*

Despite all of the drama of the full year before, which was 2007, the summer 2008, really was one in a lifetime occasion. There were three reunions scheduled all for the week before and of the 4th of July.

SVT Reunion

There was the Sadie V. Thompson Era Reunion. For those readers who are confused. This is how we all got together with the students who were segregated as, *Black only* until 1976.

Since schools were integrated in 1976 all students who attended school at the last new Black high school come together for a reunion every three years. This time of attending Sadie V. Thompson High School along with the Black students who went to the segregated private school and the county high school at Natchez College established a foundation and restored the Sadie V. Thompson High School Facility as a community center. It is no longer a school, because the white students were not going to attend this Black school even if they lived in the neighborhood when there was forced integration of all students in Natchez, Mississippi. Instead, all black students had to attend the *White High Schools* on Highway 61 and in the white residential neighborhoods. They left the middle and elementary schools as they were but when students got to high school, there was integration by fact that there was no other school to attend. Even then, the social occasions were separate. There were two proms and two sets of queens and two sets of this and divided so that it was only the physical plants and the sports teams that were integrated. Blacks and Whites got to know and appreciate each other for which they were . . . individuals as one of the positives from integration. This has advanced substantially over the ensuring years. However, the number of individuals who attended the segregated schools from 1954 to 1976 had a kinship and connection. This timeframe is known as the, SVT Era.

The numbers of attendees are dwindling over the years yet the zeal is still there. Participants return from all over the nation to attend and celebrate together. They come from those special times of in living in Mississippi when being black was all that they had and there was no other choice. Black students only had each other to network with and relate to. The irony of it all is that the reunions are boosting the economy of the city of Natchez. Black citizens are doing for the economy what they never could have experienced when there was segregation.

When all of these black citizens come back they bring their families and some their extended families. This influx of patrons and individuals fill the new hotels that had been built to accommodate just such commerce. There was the new convention center that was used for reunions, weddings and social gatherings that would have never happened during the timeframe of segregation. The historical Eola Hotel would not have allowed us inside even if we had paid double during my school years.

Yet, today you and I can make reservations and linger as paying guests with the same privileges as any other guest. You can figure the income that is now being generated by those lucrative, SVT *Era* and class reunions which are held yearly because there are always a class year or family reunion to celebrate in Natchez, Mississippi.

Beverly Family Reunion

Then there was the Beverly Family Reunion which is my dad's maternal family roots. This is the family of Mama Tex, Mrs.

Texanna White. Her dad was a Beverly. The Beverly's, spans the United States and has held reunions that we attended in Chicago, and Bloomington, Illinois; as well as San Antonio, Texas along with celebrations in Lake St. John, just north of Ferriday, Louisiana. The majority of the Beverly Reunions are hosted in Ferriday, Louisiana where the oldest family member still lives. This is Mrs. Rosie Elaine who lived with Mama Tex for a time while she was a teenager. She is now the owner of the property that once belonged to her mom, Aunt Lucille who supplied my goodies that I carried to college in my suitcases. She took over her cousins, the Beverly-Tennessee family's properties that she is still caring for. Cousin Rosie has the space and heart to host the many reunions and gatherings for family as they venture home to Ferriday, Natchez and the Miss-Lou area. The free space and communities close enough to enjoy for days at a time makes the Beverly Reunions even more desirable when hosted by Cousin Rosie. We also attended this one in the summer of 2008. I am the next in line for the linage of the Beverly family right next to cousin Rosie our loving Elder.

Families in both Reunions

It just happened that the Beverly Reunion was in Ferriday which was twenty miles from the White Family Reunion during the same week. The Beverly Reunion got as much of our time as the White Reunion with attendance at both of the church services also. The best part of the Beverly Reunion was the special photo booklet that every family was given for a special fee. It is a keepsake and it really covered the entire event in photos that can be shared for generations to come. This is true of the love and connections of the Beverly Family because Rosie has the same nature as our grandmother, Mrs. Texanna White. Earlier in my story, I shared that Rosie who was also Mama Tex's granddaughter and stayed a short while in the White's family home as a girl. Because Cousin Rosie is so accommodating, we are all very appreciative. Reunions are great ways to get together and seek long lasting family ties. Life after all is a journey or when you consider the younger generation meeting the older generation it really can be a destiny.

The White Family Reunion

Finally there was the White's Family Reunion which had its roots from my mother's paternal family line. This Wilson, White and Netterville reunion was huge in that it was started from my granddad's grandmother, Irene Wilson who was at the Whitehall Plantation south of Vidalia, Louisiana. The White Family reunion was derived from my granddad's mother, Celestine who was one of Irene children. Irene produced three branches of families. I always thought that the White's were the only descendants from my great grandmother, whom I knew as, Mama Tina. Her name was Celestine Wilson White. My great grandmother, Celestine had Wilson and Netterville siblings. With research before the White family reunion, first of many we were able to put all of this information together, what a task and what a celebration we were able to have in the Miss-Lou area. Irene was not a slave but a free black woman. All of my life, I knew about Whitehall because of cousins who continued to live in the old sharecropper homes that lined the roadway south of the Plantation. There was a Whitehall cemetery that all of our White family, ancestors who were black were buried in. There was also a different cemetery for the white ancestors at Whitehall. It was only in 2008 that it all came together as individuals, cousins and our large group of relatives. It is such a wonderful feeling to be connected to so many and learn more of the roots generated by my Great-great-grandmother, Irene Wilson.

Irene Wilson was the first known member of our line of descendants. The 2008 reunion was an organized, researched family reunion. The roots are deep and the branches full. The occasion was more than rewarding because over a year many of us connected via e-mail as we did the search. It was so rewarding to be together with all of the responders and ones who contacted us to share their family information. We were able to mingle as we acquainted, and some re-acquainted making it a very awesome experience. The reunion was truly worth the trip of coming home to Mississippi. For me personally, with the help of several of the older male cousins, I was able to run the generations of the White, Wilson and Netterville family down to the sixth generation. It is an awesome documentation and one that has future built all in and around it. It truly was rewarding to meet and put the names and faces together. The White's reunion will grow and grow because today so many of us are connected by social networking, e-mail and the love of just being able to contact family all over the United States of America.

Commerce, Culture and Change

The area of Natchez and Vidalia are divided by the Mississippi River. Natchez and Adams County on the east side of the

Mississippi river. Vidalia and Concordia Parish on the west side of the Mississippi river. Between the two areas are two bridges and development of great commerce. There are several Casino Boats that support gambling. Hotels have been built on both sides of the river. On both sides are convention centers and entertainment facilities. One of the largest economic boosters is the ongoing return of tourism and citizens who left the area in the Jim Crow Era to seek a better livelihood.

Every year, thousands of former citizens and their families flock to the Miss-Lou area for family reunions. The continuing reunions are a time to reconnect with family and the past for those who left. They all left because Mississippi did not provide the economic, social and even the educational support for this once younger generation. Now as their finances have improved, social and justice restraints have become inclusive, the once *Negros* are welcome and capable of making the revered Pilgrimage every couple of years back to Mississippi and the area around the Mississippi River.

There are two states but one area in, The *Miss-Lou area.* The roots of commerce are already defined in banking, touring, and culture. There is a long history of the people who live and work there as well as those who left as we did and make a pilgrimage back home at least annually. The Miss-Lou area is where many who left now return and help to boost the economy with the finances they earned because they could not earn this kind of life had they remained in the Miss-Lou or the segregated Mississippi.

The prior Slavery and plantation history is alive with its economic structures as well as the major income generated with the present, River Boat Casino Resorts. Due to their close proximity the Miss-Lou area is striving in spite of prior plant and industry closures. Natchez is positioned as the retirement hub on the Mississippi River. Many family members have taken the offer and made a home back in the Miss-Lou area. Not only are the reunions successful but seem to fuel the attendees to come back permanently to a place that they previously escaped. Even I have thought about the idea. But it is family and the medical services I enjoy that keep me here in California. Yet, I continue to be drawn year to year, back to Mississippi.

Natchez has enormous, *old money* and has seen new interest and venues as it provides services and provisions under the twenty first century city directors. I may not be a permanent resident of Mississippi, but there is the draw of family and the continued improvement that keeps us going back. The attitude of the citizens in general has improved with the economy. The good ole boys mentality have slowly softened to include the new attitude that a man is a man, not to be judged or appreciated by the color of his skin, his culture or ancestry but by the ability that is innate. Further demonstrating that what is developed by the education or capabilities allowed to all men and women are the rights of all citizens. It is a life time journey, one that changed for the better. This journey is not yet final, but certainly one to be reckoned with as we make our way back to Mississippi. Residents and reunion attendees can see that there is more tolerance and acceptance of diverse cultures in the state of Mississippi. A change from the segregated era is welcomed with open arms.

Mississippi has a rich history, and heritage. This attribute was evident in the segregated state but it was appreciated as blacks left the south and shared their talents and skills abroad for the world to see. Even with individuals like me, I have learned that I am appreciated less by those who claim to know me best. Now we know that the Mississippi area and region is one of the largest historical areas in the south. A good example of this history that is probably least known in Natchez but so very popular is the Trace.

The Natchez Trace Parkway runs 444 miles from Natchez to Nashville and is more than 8,000 years old. It was a path traced out by the buffalo and later the road was traveled by traders, missionaries, early settlers, and Indians. It became a connected roadway with improved lanes just a few years ago. I had the pleasure of observing this improvement as I returned and observed the changes made on the Natchez Trace because this is the point where it begins in moving to the north. Mississippi and Louisiana also have a rich history in the arts. It is said that Mississippi is the birthplace of American music. The blues, gospel, country and rock 'n roll all had roots here in Mississippi. I witnessed the Blues dominance in the small town of Ferriday, LA which is just west of Vidalia and in the same Parish. I am blessed to say that I was there as a young woman in much of this historical beginning. The Haney's Big House is the biggest recognized place in the history of this part of the Miss-Lou Area. Inside of the walls of Haney's Big House or House of Blues as it was called you could find well known stars. There were celebrities as well known as B.B. King, Muddy Waters, Jackie Wilson, Wilson Pickett, and even James Brown. Many of the reunion attendees knew of these artistic contributors even before they left the south for the financial resources of the North and West Coast. Those were just a few of the artists highlighted during the years at this black owned and operated house of music.

Mississippi boasts many writers and actors, among them are Morgan Freeman and Oprah Winfrey. Those two Mississippians are only two out of those who came from Mississippi and made a dynamic change for humankind in their own life contributions. Morgan Freeman came back to Mississippi and made his home in the Delta region. Jackson, Mississippi the state capital where the first integration occurred and hosts several local and professional theater companies. The Summers Hotel Blues Spot is one of them and continues to provide great memoirs for those who are cultural seekers.

Natchez holds its own as the primary place for the Old South Pilgrimage which happens twice a year. This has been a long time financial support for the Miss-Lou area. With the tourist trade, add the food which is a gastronomic experience. Here is where deep fried catfish continue to be king in many eateries. Fishing in the state of Louisiana and designates it as the sportsmen's paradise.

Stately Antebellum homes blossom on vast groomed properties from the bygone era of slavery and the Civil War. So you can see that the cultural side in Mississippi has and continue to have a lot to offer many. In the past twenty to thirty years blacks found employment in all of these areas and have a decent living. Prior to the Tougaloo Nine and the subsequent integration, blacks were only allowed to be cooks, laundry, ground keepers and other unskilled jobs in the factories. Now you find blacks in managerial, white collar and civic positions all over the state. The state is now visually run and supported by blacks in all areas of commerce. Thanks to the results of civil unrest and civil rights victory in Mississippi all citizens can now pursue whatever skills they may choose as a career.

Coming home to Natchez, Mississippi and the Miss-Lou area is a powerful acknowledgement for me. When I was a teen I did not have the opportunities to enjoy a choice of schools and facilities such as the Convention Centers that my family members now embrace and enjoy. While at the 2008 Reunion Picnic, for the White's Family held at the Veterans of Foreign Wars (VFW) near the Super Wal-Mart, we were welcomed and spent opportune time in peace and security. This was not always a normal occurrence in this Miss-Lou area. Because of the contributions of the Tougaloo Nine students, advancement in the struggle for human rights was brought to an all time high and important moment in our state's history. Today, the green canopy of magnolia trees, the magnificent vines that grow along the Highway 61 and the Pine trees that grow and provides soft wood for the paper mills gives one the tranquility that was unheard of for all citizens before March 27, 1961.

One of my cousins came up to me at our, 2008 Family Reunion and gave me the greatest honor by acknowledging that my efforts as a college student opened the doors in Mississippi, March 27, 1961 for all men and women to enjoy. This and many other opportunities are now taken for granted. This is because of not knowing the history of what was! To obtain the freedom to enjoy the facilities and financial strides were made because of great sacrifices made in the form of civil unrest. Now, peace and fellowship ensues in most communities, towns and cities in the historical State of Mississippi.

As a student at Tougaloo College I was one of the students known as the Tougaloo Nine. I keep telling you this because this manuscript is my platform for acknowledging the fact that we breached the doors of the all white public library in Jackson, Mississippi. Many individuals do not know or care about this event because they never experienced the forced injustice we had to live in as a way of life. Every time that I am validated for what we did, I am essentially screaming to you to remember this history. What we did was to be forever locked in the history that, we opened the doors not just to the Jackson Library but to all public and private venues, facilities, policies and life in general in the state of Mississippi. Black residents and reunion attendees all make the state of Mississippi economy grow. For these annual pilgrimages with the return of black citizens the State of Mississippi should be grateful and appreciative. I wonder if they really realize this fact.

Part 14:
A Journey or Destiny?

Chapter 28

Where do we go from here?

My fellow school mates and I opened the doors of opportunity to Mississippi and the Miss-Lou area for the posterity of generations to come. I am humbled to share with you the true meaning of this prestigious place in my life. As members of today's society there are still lots of concerns. Many concerns have to do with the fact that this *world* in which we now live is *speeding faster than, we can keep up with it*. Taking out time to reflect on the past and see our future in the person of our younger family members were quite evident to me as I experienced our very first, White Family Reunion in 2008. The Theme was *The first of many*!

The first of many happened because of the efforts of a few relatives. When will there be another? We hope that it happens while some of us can still make the trip. During the celebration, I found what was expressed by Houston Chronicle Journalist, Ana Veceana-Suarez to be applicable to the now generation. She wrote in her article about baby boomers that express where we are as multi-populations. As we know, Boomers are our largest population group now! I have passed this generation in age but found myself in the situation by virtue of the fact that I had to take care of my adopted parents and at the same time support my daughter and granddaughter. I understood this statement because it was what

I had to experience firsthand. The younger generation has much to do to overcome the stresses and pressures put upon the body by just being in the place where we are. *We are a generation that has more money, less time for vacations, responsibility of elderly parents who are living longer and our children as well!*

In order to benefit from an ideal life it will take a change in our present thinking pattern. First, maximize our assets and minimize our liabilities. This change can happen by re-adjusting our attitudes as Ms Veceana-Suarez suggested. I concur with her suggestion that as citizens, *we can find the satisfaction of living with just enough.* More important she further stressed, how *we can discover the moment or attitude in our life where gratitude meets acceptance.* This is really, what the writing of, *Back to Mississippi* is all about? We must discover the mindset where gratitude meets acceptance for who we are and what our capabilities are. We can now have expectations that fit perfectly within our grasp. The lifestyle that I lived as a youngster, denies me the rights to do what I wanted to accomplish, yet I found a way around many of the restraints. Included in restraints were the skating in my neighborhood, the ability to ride a bike in a safe area and even the ability to receive dance classes. The civil disobedience, which I participated in, was to make life better for me and citizens like me. Because of what I was able to do opened avenues of higher learning, political offices, voting for all citizens and so many other previously denied privileges. We are blessed each day that we are given, to experience life to its fullest. We should not dwell on the past for it is long gone. I am not saying, to not remember the past. Thank you for reading my memories of what was for me and my realization of what I accomplished. Through the exercise of sharing my feelings and experiences I can say you helped me to open up and let it be known that I feel vindicated among my other received gestures. Those gestures of approval, appreciation and acknowledgment have been healing and at the same time, let me plant seeds of confidence for you to consider.

It has been well documented that if you do not know your past you are positioned to repeat it. I plead with you to not dwell on the future because it is just that, a place and time that you have yet to see. It is prudent, however, that you plan for the future. Time and history has proven that if you fail to plan, you plan to fail. The future is definitely a time to look forward to.

I say without hesitation to you, plan ahead and keep your options positive. You can do or be as productive as you think you can. To do this you must concurrently affirm that you can. I know that my experience with the Tougaloo Nine was all about taking a stand to do or just to say within, *I can*! I did it and you can also; just enjoy life as you live in the present. Keep your mind focused on where you are and learn to enjoy the moment. It is attainable to love who you are! It is feasible to live in your present situation or to change it by changing where you are or how you feel about where you are. I love to share how to experience the moment because your present state of being is best when you learn to be grateful. Success can be accomplished when you continue to accept yourself as a powerful presence of being. Keep your mind in the present and your expectations within your own reach, not to be measured by someone else. When you follow this ideology, you are not stressed and can find peace which is within your grasp. Peace is very possible when you live in the presence.

Living in the present is just that, because we are thinking individuals we are swayed by our past and motivated by our goals for our future. We must be aware of the morale and cultures while utilizing the assets and abilities that we are given. We must remember what can and has been acquired up to this present moment.

There is a very clearly defined story about life that I love to read over and over as well as share. The story is one of those children tales about the ant and the grasshopper from Aesop Fables. You may not know or ever heard of Aesop's fables. The book may not be in print but if it is and you have the opportunity to read it, you just may see yourself in that fable. The ant is industrious, hard working, a team player and knows what is required to prepare for its future. The grasshopper on the other hand, is a loner, fun loving, player who enjoys living for today and now; without any thought for the future. Both of these descriptions are acceptable lifestyles but do they work for you in your goals. Living in the present is good. Do you know how to live for your best lifetime as your choice? The fable of the ant and the grasshopper describes in a simple story the connections of past knowledge, present participation and future expectations. They both show that the choice you make determines your real destiny. Your destiny is in your hands; you can say yes to life and enjoy it.

While riding my cousin's bicycle I made the choice to turn to the right when I crossed the bridge that spanned the ditch. Had, I chosen the turn to the left, there was the strong possibility that I may have run into the low hanging branches of the willow tree. This decision would have taken me only 300 feet towards a barbed wire fence that protected the cotton field. Besides, I would not have been able to stop or start the bike. When I considered the choice of direction I chose to take, I secured the fact that my short journey was a safe one rather than a disaster that may have resulted in bruised or even broken limbs.

When I made the choice 50 years ago to be a part of a *historical life changing event*, I had to accept the consequences. Life took on the enactment of how my life played out many years ago. You can step up to the plate of accomplishment and determine your own destiny. In Vidalia, I traveled alone, but I was not lonely. I had a wonderful family life that was filled with love, protection and most of all, circumstances that helped me make choices early in life. As I skated on the sidewalks from the black neighborhood, through the white neighborhood, I had a destiny. My destiny was to get to the place where I could freely experience my God given skill and exercise my ability to safely go where no one else in my family had attempted to go. This was the beginning of my life explorations and there were many to come. I made steps for accomplishments at every part of my life journey. I traveled the path that was paved for smooth skating. I saw my goal and set my sights on it. It was complicated at times as the steps of the courthouse stairs that I safely scaled. Through all of the steps I made, it was with a purpose. Sometimes this purpose was clear, and sometime it was cloudy and the fine line was not something that I could be sure of. As I developed my spiritual self and let go of my physical self, I learned that there was something called, Faith.

I found that this one step of faith was a solid one and worthy of holding on to for eternity. No matter where I have been, or even where I am, I hold fast to the thought that there is a better life out there for me. Thinking in the positive can work well for you, as it has for me. Life is a journey, are you leading or following? Your destiny is like the decision for me of going back to Mississippi, because of the choices that made it a much more receptive state for blacks and all other citizens.

We must acknowledge those who struggled to gain social change here in our nation. You may not know who struggled for this change. Please know, they all said, *I can*! We, the members of the Tougaloo Nine knew the past; we acted in the present, to make a change for the future. We had a desire for a future more accountable to all human kind in their future. We knew that *freedom* had a price and we stepped up to proclaim by our actions. *I can make a difference in what was and what can be!*

To go back to Mississippi today in peace and justice as a citizen is easier, desirable and highly attainable. People will be people in every state of these United States. Mississippi started for me with segregation, intimidation, injustice, second class citizenship, degraded educational materials; lynching's and devalued pay for skilled and unskilled labor, while the whites enjoyed feelings of superiority. However, after all of the years, I have returned to Mississippi for a family visit or reunions, *The hospitality seems to be genuine*. There may be haters and those who have regret for the formulation of life in general but my story has shown that given the opportunity there can be victory, for all who diligently seek it!

I have witnessed in the last decade, attitudes I never imagined as a youngster growing up in the turn of the mid-century of integration, inclusion, employment, not only the right to vote but black politicians, congressmen and women, managers of major businesses, hotel and restaurant owners and CEO's as well. There are many achievers in all areas of life including people who look like me in every facet of business. Looking in from my point of view, Mississippi has made a 180 degree turn around for living life in optimum freedom. Mississippi provides the ability to live and grow in education, political and economical areas within the constitutional allowances. An individual is not held down or back because of their ethnicity but by the will to do better. If what is desired cannot be obtained in one community, there is the opportunity to go where you can be successful as my family did. In the future, I pray that the residential areas and public housing divide in the state of Mississippi are pulled together. There are still large pockets of segregated residential areas. When that change in living where you can afford to happens, we can truly say, *"Mississippi is truly worthy of revisiting or making a final trip, Back to Mississippi"!* I was a resident of the state of Mississippi. I remain a returnee to Mississippi. I know who I am. I know where I am going. I leave you with the question, only you can answer or justify. Is the trip worth the journey? Can you live your life in peace after the struggles I made and see the possibilities for generations to come? As you visualize my story, make the virtual visit then conceptualize your own destiny in my story about, "Back to Mississippi".

Appendix: The Year-long Program of the 45th Anniversary of the Tougaloo Nine and the 2006 Educational Program with comments.

Appendix

The yearlong Program

Wednesday, April 5, 2006 6:00—7:30 p. m.

"Celebrating the Jackson Movement" (Jackson State University included Comments and Greetings by President Ron Mason and Tougaloo President Beverly Hogan (*who is also an alumna of Tougaloo*). Images of the Jackson Movement were shown on a projection screen. Roundtable Discussions: The Origins and Impact of the Jackson Movement," moderated by Dr. Leslie McLemore, featuring Jackson Movement veterans James "Sam" Bradford, (One of the Tougaloo Nine), Frankye Adams-Johnson, Jimmie Travis, and Hollis Watkins.

Wednesday June 14, 2006 7:00-8:30 p.m.

Panel Discussion and Audience Q&A at Jackson State University. "The Coming of the Freedom Riders: A Movement Builds Momentum" Participants: Mr. Dave Dennis, former Freedom Rider and current Director of the Southern Initiative of the Algebra Project; former Freedom Riders Mr. Jerome Smith, and Mr. Hank Thomas, Mr. Belton Cox, and Ms. Carol Ruth Silver.

(This happened in the summer of 1961 after the Tougaloo Nine Library Sit-In. This action was a direct reaction of the Tougaloo Nine who inspired students at other campuses to see that they too could try to change the state's segregation laws and mentality.)

Wednesday August 9, 2006 7:00-8:30 p.m.

Panel Discussion (Tougaloo College, Woodworth Chapel)

"Area College Students in the Freedom Struggle: The Role of the NAACP's Youth Chapter"

Moderator: Professor Charles H. Holmes, Pre-Law Advisor, Tougaloo College Panelists: Mr. James "Sam" Bradford, community leader and member of the Tougaloo Nine, Ms. Constance Slaughter-Harvey, former Assistant Secretary of State, Mississippi, Dr. Hollis Watkins, President, Southern Echo, Inc., Dr. Gene Young, community leader, Mr. Malcolm shepherd, local businessman, Ms. Frankye Adams-Johnson, Instructor, Department of English, JSU, Dr. T.W. Lewis, Professor of Religion (ret.), Millsap's College

Friday, September 8, 2006 7:00-8:00 p.m. Reception and Photo Exhibit (Eudora Welty Public Library) Photographs of the Tougaloo Nine and the Jackson Movement from the Mississippi Department of Archives and History. *(From me: if you do not know your History . . .)*

Thursday, October 5, 2006 6:00-8:00 p.m.

23rd Annual Fannie Lou Hamer Memorial Symposium Lecture Series

(Jackson State University) "JSU and Campbell College Students in the Jackson Movement" (*As you can see . . . History!!!*) Moderator: Sr. Robert Walker, Chief Administrative Officer, City of Jackson and Visiting Assistant Professor of History, Jackson State University Panelists: Dr. ivory Phillips, Dean, College of Education, JSU, Dr. EC Foster, Professor of History (ret.), JSU, Dr. Velvelyn Foster, Acting Vice President of Academic Affairs, JSU, Mr. Dave Dennis, Director of the Southern Initiative of The Algebra Project, Ms. Minnie Watson, Curator, Medgar Evers Home & Museum.

Friday, October 6, 2006 9:30 a.m.

Focus on Jackson High Schools (Campus of Lanier High School)

Keynote Address: Dr. Robert Moses Director, The Algebra Project 9:30-11:00 a.m.

"Student Participation from Jackson to Mc Comb" Respondents: Mr. Dave Dennis, Director, The Southern Initiative of the Algebra Project Dr. Gene Young, **Community Leader**, **Mr. Jimmie Travis, Community Leader**

Freedom Songs led by Dr. Hollis Watkins, yard of LHS 11:00 a.m.

Wednesday, October 11, 2006 7:30 p.m.-8:30 p.m.

Tougaloo College Founder's Week Presidential Lecture (Woodworth Chapel)

Ms. Dorie Lander, social worker and civil rights veteran "The Jackson Movement in Retrospect"

Friday, October 13, 2006 5:00-6:30 p.m. Keynote Address (Smith Robertson Museum and Cultural Center) 5:00-6:30 p.m. Dr. John Dittmer, Professor of History (ret.) DePauw University

"The Historical Context and Significance of the Jackson Movement"

(Note: Dorie was one of the Jackson College students suspended for their Prayer Vigil, when we, the Tougaloo Nine was arrested for the Jackson Library Sit-In)

The Newspaper clips were from the Newspaper input after in anticipation of our Recognition and Participation in the Panel Discussions at Tougaloo College.

"The Clarion-Ledger front page Highlights, Jackson Honors Tougaloo Nine . . . Though the Tougaloo Nine's recollections of March 27, 1961, vary, their actions indisputably helped trigger the civil rights movement in Jackson.

And tonight the nine former Tougaloo College students will be given keys to the city that once shut them out socially and economically.

. . ."*It's a wonderful opportunity to walk about Jackson's streets and have somebody smile*" (Omar, Now Deceased)

After tonight's event at Tougaloo's Alumni banquet, the group will recount that day in a panel discussion from 9:30 a.m. to 4:p.m Saturday in Woodworth Chapel on Campus.

"*This is clearly something that the city should have done a long time ago,*" *said Leslie B. McLemore, a Jackson city councilman and director of the Fannie Lou Hamer National Institute on Citizenship and Democracy at Jackson State University. The Institute is an event co-sponsor.*

The group's (Tougaloo Nine) actions reverberated throughout Mississippi, McLemore said.

Students at other campuses saw that they could try to change the state's segregation."

Saturday October 14, 2006 9:00 a.m.-11:00 a.m. Tougaloo College, Woodworth Chapel

Panelist: Members of Tougaloo Nine Look Back at Historic Day!

This session was both traumatic and exciting for me as I sat with my fellow Tougaloo Nine group and remembered how it really felt on the day and following experiences.

Participants: Moderator, Reverend Ed King, Ms. Geraldine Edwards Hollis, Mr. James "Sam" Bradford, Mr. Albert Lassiter, and Dr. Evelyn Pierce Omar via telephone (*Deceased*)

It was wonderful to be back in Woodworth Chapel which is one of the most inclusive Venues on the Tougaloo Campus. To speak to my peers, professors and students along with dignitaries to come out to support this continuation of History from our point of view was refreshing and an honor.

WLBT 3 on your side, by Cheryl Lasseter, "Do you know the story of the Tougaloo Nine? It's a big part of Mississippi's history. The efforts of nine college students 45 years ago made a big difference in the civil rights movement, and this weekend some of those students gathered for a reunion on campus.

"If only the trees on the Tougaloo College campus could talk." James Bradford says he's sure they would bring even more perspective to the incident that's put the Tougaloo Nine in the history books.

"There are as many stories and experts as there are individuals who just lived during those times," he said..

On March 27th 1961, Bradford was one of nine Tougaloo students who executed a carefully planned but daring move. The students walked into the Jackson Municipal Library, which blacks were prohibited from entering, and began to study. Jackson police soon moved in and arrested them and they were jailed for 32 hours. The Tougaloo Nine-four women and five men –touched off the manor movement in the city of Jackson toward civil rights. Forty five years later several members of the Tougaloo Nine gather at the campus's historic Woodworth Chapel to recall their experiences. Geraldine Edwards Hollis says in her family she always did things first.

"The first to go to college, the first to do everything, I was the first to go to jail. Ha, ha," expressed Hollis. (Although I could laugh at that time, the experience was not laughing matter. It was a big risk both for me and for my family. My education and future career was riding on the results of my participation in this civil disobedience. But, it was something, my life experiences had prepared me for, to make a difference in my life and my family as well as those around me. We are thankful, to the media coverage of WLBT 3 on your side, and by Ms Cheryl Lasseter. Also to James "Sam" Bradford who is there in the Jackson Area and able to speak representing the Tougaloo Nine, as the rest are spread all over the United States.)

Panel Two: 1:00 p.m.-4:30 p.m. Woodworth Chapel

Moderator: Professor Richard (Dick) Johnson, Ms. Ethel Sawyer Adolphe, Mr. Meredith Anding, Jr., Ms. Janice Jackson Vails and Mr. Alfred Cook.

All participants were given a chance to express their views looking back on that historical event. "The contributions of this group of brave students helped to advance the struggle for human rights, and documented an important moment in our state's history. The panel discussion is the finale of the ongoing events held throughout the year celebrating the noteworthy contributions of youth to the Jackson Civil Rights Movement. The Tougaloo Community . . . welcome home these icons of civic engagement one of the tenets this College holds so dear. (Tougaloo College Office of Institutional Advancement)

Resources: To Explore the Jackson-Area Civil Rights Movement

1. Brochure, "If you're Gon ' Be a Leader, Don't Stay Behind"_ remembering the Jackson Civil Rights Movement. October 14, 2006

2. Hamer Happenings, The Newsletter of the Fannie Lou Hamer National Institute on Citizenship and Democracy. Volume 9, No. 1 Winter 2006

3. Jackson Honors Tougaloo Nine. Laura Hipp, "From locked cells to keys to city", The Clarion-Ledger. Jackson 10/13/06

4. Mississippi Digital Library. Tougaloo College. Hosted by USM Libraries   *http://collections.msdiglib.org/cdm4*   11/15/2010 Articles: Dr. A.D. Beittel; inventory of the Office of Public Relations-Ruth Owens; John Mangram, Chaplin of TC 1950-1961, Advisor to Tougaloo Nine, Inventory of The John Mangram Papers; Letter of Support from Dr. A.D. Beittel. 04/19/1961; Medger Wiley Evers 1925-1963.

5. Members of Tougaloo Nine, Look Back at Historical Day. Cheryl Lassiter, WLBT3, On your Side. Tougaloo 10/14/06

6. Mississippi Heritage Trust-Jackson, MS. *www. mississippiheritage.com* 11/15/2010

7. Mississippi Report, "Jackson Reaches Turning Point". The Southern Patriot, vol. 19, No. 5 May, 1961

8. New Programs to Explore The Jackson-Area Civil Rights Movement. Mississippi Digital Library. *http://collections. msdiglib.org/cdm4* 11/15/10

9. Tougaloo Nine Honored 45 Years Later. Cheryl Lassiter, WLBT 3 On Your Side. Jackson, MS 03/27/06

10. Web Links to refer to:

Direct action or Voter registration
Geraldine Hollis, Jackson Library Sit-in
Jackson Municipal Library (Mississippi heritage Trust)
Mississippi. The Eye of the Storm.
Tougaloo Nine, Tougaloo College
When Youth Protest: The MS Civil Rights Movement
(MS Historical Society)